OpenAI API Cookbook

Build intelligent applications including chatbots,
virtual assistants, and content generators

Henry Habib

OpenAI API Cookbook

Group Product Manager: Niranjan Naikwadi

Publishing Product Manager: Tejashwini R

Executive Editor: Mudita S

Technical Editor: Yash Bhanushali

Copy Editor: Safis Editing

Proofreader: Safis Editing

Indexer: Hemangini Bari

Production Designers: Jyoti Kadam and Gokul Raj S.T

DevRel Marketing Coordinator: Vinishka Kalra

First published: March 2024

Production reference: 1060324

Published by
Packt Publishing Ltd.
Grosvenor House
11 St Paul's Square
Birmingham
B3 1RB, UK.

ISBN 978-1-80512-135-0

www.packtpub.com

To Soniya, Faisal, Munira, Maheen, Karan, and Riri.

– Henry

Foreword

I started working with Henry after taking one of his online courses, where he was teaching working professionals how they could save time and work faster by using no-code tools. He was both passionate and practical when delivering his content. Particularly, he focused on tangible use cases rather than abstract concepts that did not drive real-world outcomes.

Having been in the field of AI and productivity for more than 10 years, he saw the emerging *citizen developer* trend where anyone could build tools and solutions quickly without knowing any code. When the OpenAI API was first released to the public, Henry was one the first to teach professionals how they can use it to work faster, and his course quickly reached *bestseller* status within one week of its release.

In this book, Henry takes you on a journey on how to use the OpenAI API to build intelligent applications – tools that you can use to automate processes, improve productivity, save time, or build new businesses. He starts by introducing the OpenAI API and its endpoints, features, and parameters, and then he uses it to build apps and assistants. Throughout the book, he always adds practical and real-life examples so that you can start creating an impact from the first page.

This is an essential guide for knowledge workers eager to harness the power of OpenAI and ChatGPT to build intelligent applications and solutions. It enables you to integrate the OpenAI API into various domains, from simple apps to whole assistants.

Henry is also the architect behind *The Intelligent Worker*, one of the largest newsletters focused on teaching everyday workers how they can be productive at work with AI, automation, no-code, and other technologies. He continues his mission to empower individuals and boost their productivity through technologies with his online courses.

Sam McKay, CEO and founder of Enterprise DNA, which offers top-notch data and AI skills training to over 220,000 data professionals

Today, AI and ChatGPT are much more than household words, being a consistent and animated point of discussion and debate. However, they are also immediately actionable tools that can deliver a mind-bending list of potential applications. Unlike any technology in history, AI (and ChatGPT) has eclipsed traditional milestones in user usage, spurring spectacular growth from application ideas through to development and deployment.

For people like you (and me), who are interested in implementing ChatGPT in new and innovative ways, ChatGPT's meteoric rise to prominence is a testament to the relevance of the problems it solves, and to the importance that information and tools play in today's digital society. With its unparalleled ability to understand and generate human-like text, ChatGPT represents not just a technological leap but a paradigm shift in human-computer interaction.

As you journey through this book, I strongly encourage you to take copious notes and to use it as the working handbook that Henry Habib intended it to be. Use it to create your next successful app or business, or employ it to enrich your thinking about how to innovate your next great thing. In fact, I hope you will do what any successful entrepreneur, innovator, investor, or developer does when they are presented with a lot of information and opportunity – *dream on it*. That's right – take the ideas and information you gain in this book and *dream on it*. Then, return to the book again and again to fashion your dreams into a reality with the tools you will have gained here.

I believe Henry has masterfully constructed *OpenAI API Cookbook*. But I knew he could and would when I first learned of this project. From the day Henry and I first met, I recognized in him an impressive combination of technical expertise and communications skills. As a result, I have engaged him in professional development and educational programs for a global network of enterprises (including HSBC) and online education platforms (including Coursera). His proficiency in tools such as SQL, Python, Spark, Qlik Sense, and TensorFlow, combined with his practical knowledge of big data analysis in financial services, retail, and telecommunications, his underlining passion for AI and machine learning, and his ability to communicate simply make him an ideal author to create this guidebook.

I know you will thoroughly enjoy this book, as I did. Use it, as I have, and see your next dream come true.

Paul Siegel, serial technology entrepreneur and CEO and founder of Starweaver, a top-tier education platform focused on technology and business

Contributors

About the author

Henry Habib is a manager at one of the world's top management consulting firms, advising F500 companies on analytics and operations, with a particular focus on building intelligent AI-driven solutions and tools to create impact. He is a passionate online instructor and educator, amassing a network of more than 150,000 paid students and facilitating technical programs at large banks and governmental organizations.

A proponent of the no-code and LLM revolution, he believes that anyone can now create powerful and intelligent applications without any deep technical skills. Henry resides in Toronto, Canada, with his wife, and he enjoys reading AI research papers and playing tennis in his free time.

I want to thank Mudita, Tejashwini, and the Packt team for helping me expand my passion for education to the written medium.

About the reviewers

Arindam Ganguly has been working as an experienced data scientist at one of the leading multi-national software service firms for more than eight years, where he is responsible for developing and designing intelligent solutions, leveraging his expertise in AI and data analytics. He also has a vast amount of expertise in developing automation and hyper-automation solutions, leveraging automated workflow engines, and integrating them with AI.

Arindam is also a published author, writing the book *Build and Deploy Machine Learning Solutions Using IBM Watson*, which teaches you how to build AI applications using the popular IBM Watson toolkit.

Ashutosh Vishwakarma is the co-founder of `Verifast.tech`, a pioneering conversational AI firm, and he has over eight years of expertise in developing and architecting high-scale, machine learning-driven systems. He spearheads innovations within the **Large Language Model** (**LLM**) ecosystem, focusing on crafting next-generation user experiences. His comprehensive background ensures a deep understanding of both the technical and strategic facets of AI development, from conception to deployment.

Eswari Jayakumar is a passionate software developer with over seven years of experience, proficient in multiple programming languages. Her expertise spans a wide array of technologies, with a profound interest in cutting-edge fields such as DevOps, machine learning, computer vision, and LLMs. Originally from India, she moved to Canada to pursue her master's in computer science at the University of New Brunswick. In addition to her technical acumen, Eswari is an adept content writer, sharing her technical knowledge through engaging blogs. She spends her free time volunteering in coding communities. Follow her journey and connect with her on LinkedIn (`www.linkedin.com/in/eswarijayakumar`).

Table of Contents

3

Understanding Key Parameters and Their Impact on Generated Responses   37

4

Incorporating Additional Features from the OpenAI API   55

5

Staging the OpenAI API for Application Development   75

6

Building Intelligent Applications with the OpenAI API   97

7

Building Assistants with the OpenAI API   133

Index   165

Other Books You May Enjoy   170

Preface

In the rapidly advancing generative AI world, the ability to create innovative applications such as chatbots, virtual assistants, content generation tools, and productivity enhancers can be a game-changer. The OpenAI API is your key to achieving this, enabling you to build high-performance intelligent applications in diverse industries or to increase your productivity by adding ChatGPT into your workflows.

You will begin with the fundamentals of the OpenAI API, including setup, authentication, and key parameters, enabling a solid foundation for working with API.

Next, you will learn about the different elements of the OpenAI API and how to use it effectively, along with the importance of tweaking certain parameters for better results. You will uncover extra features of the OpenAI API that will improve user experience and enable you to obtain refined outputs. Further, you will be guided on moving from development to a live application; you will learn how to set up the API for public use and application backends. Subsequently, you will be able to build knowledge-based assistants and multi-model applications that are tailored to your specific needs.

By the end of this book, you will have a comprehensive and practical mastery of the OpenAI API and will be ready to build intelligent and AI-powered solutions.

Who this book is for

This book is perfect for working professionals and citizen developers who are keen on using and mastering the OpenAI API. Ideal for quickly creating intelligent applications such as chatbots or content generators, it caters to both beginners and experienced professionals.

The OpenAI API in this book is accessed with Python. Familiarity with Python and APIs is desired but absolutely not required.

What this book covers

Chapter 1, Unlocking OpenAI and Setting Up Your API Playground Environment, covers the steps required to start working with the API and the OpenAI API Playground.

Chapter 2, OpenAI API Endpoints Explained, delves into the various endpoints available in the OpenAI API, with practical examples and use cases.

Chapter 3, Understanding Key Parameters and Their Impact on Generated Responses, discusses the significance of the key API parameters.

Chapter 4, Incorporating Additional Features from the OpenAI API, explains how to use the hidden gems of the API such as embeddings and fine-tuning.

Chapter 5, Staging the OpenAI API for Application Development, transitions from fiddling with the API to using it to build real-life applications.

Chapter 6, Building Intelligent Applications with the OpenAI API, covers how to build various different intelligent applications with the API.

Chapter 7, Building Assistants with the OpenAI API, provides a tutorial on how to build knowledge-based assistants with the API.

> This book contains many long screenshots. These have been captured to provide readers with an overview of various features. As a result, the text in these images may appear small at 100% zoom.

To get the most out of this book

This book uses Python to access the OpenAI API. Familiarity with Python is recommended to get the most out of this book, but not required as all code snippets that are used will be shared.

Since the book uses APIs, some knowledge of APIs and how they work is recommended but, again, not required.

Some basic understanding of programming concepts such as functions and loops will be needed as they will not be covered in the book.

Software/hardware covered in the book	OS requirements
Python	Windows, macOS, and Linux (any)
Postman	Windows, Mac OS X, and Linux (any)
Bubble	Windows, Mac OS X, and Linux (any)

This book leverages the OpenAI API, which you may have to pay an additional fee for if you are not eligible for the free tier. The API is charged on a per-use basis, and as a result, any misuse or abuse of the API can unintentionally result in a large invoice from OpenAI. You should always set limits on any API accounts that you create.

This book also uses Google Cloud Platform to create and deploy cloud functions, which, like the OpenAI API, can be expensive if misused. A Google account is required to access this service.

If you are using the digital version of this book, we advise you to type the code yourself or access the code via the GitHub repository (link available in the next section). Doing so will help you avoid any potential errors related to the copying and pasting of code.

Download the example code files

You can download the example code files for this book from GitHub at `https://github.com/ PacktPublishing/OpenAI-API-Cookbook`. If there's an update to the code, it will be updated on the existing GitHub repository.

We also have other code bundles from our rich catalog of books and videos available at `https:// github.com/PacktPublishing/`. Check them out!

Conventions used

There are a number of text conventions used throughout this book.

`Code in text`: Indicates code words in text, database table names, folder names, filenames, file extensions, pathnames, dummy URLs, user input, and Twitter handles. Here is an example: "In the System Message, type in the following: `You are an assistant that creates marketing slogans`."

A block of code is set as follows:

```
{
    "model": "gpt-3.5-turbo",
    "messages": [
        {
            "role": "system",
            "content": "You are an assistant that creates marketing slogans
based on descriptions of companies"
        }
```

When we wish to draw your attention to a particular part of a code block, the relevant lines or items are set in bold:

```
            "role": "assistant",
            "content": "Thank you for your kind words! Vanilla is
always a classic favorite. 😊🍦"
        },
```

Any command-line input or output is written as follows:

```
Donald Trump's presidency showcased divisive politics and tumultuous
events.
```

Bold: Indicates a new term, an important word, or words that you see onscreen. For example, words in menus or dialog boxes appear in the text like this. Here is an example: "After you have successfully logged in, navigate to **Profile** in the top right-hand menu, select **Personal**."

> **Tips or important notes**
> Appear like this.

Sections

In this book, you will find several headings that appear frequently (*Getting ready, How to do it..., How it works..., There's more...*, and *See also*).

To give clear instructions on how to complete a recipe, use these sections as follows:

Getting ready

This section tells you what to expect in the recipe and describes how to set up any software or any preliminary settings required for the recipe.

How to do it...

This section contains the steps required to follow the recipe.

How it works...

This section usually consists of a detailed explanation of what happened in the previous section.

There's more...

This section consists of additional information about the recipe in order to make you more knowledgeable about the recipe.

See also

This section provides helpful links to other useful information for the recipe.

Get in touch

Feedback from our readers is always welcome.

General feedback: If you have questions about any aspect of this book, mention the book title in the subject of your message and email us at customercare@packtpub.com.

Errata: Although we have taken every care to ensure the accuracy of our content, mistakes do happen. If you have found a mistake in this book, we would be grateful if you would report this to us. Please visit www.packtpub.com/support/errata, selecting your book, clicking on the Errata Submission Form link, and entering the details.

Piracy: If you come across any illegal copies of our works in any form on the Internet, we would be grateful if you would provide us with the location address or website name. Please contact us at copyright@packtpub.com with a link to the material.

If you are interested in becoming an author: If there is a topic that you have expertise in and you are interested in either writing or contributing to a book, please visit authors.packtpub.com.

Share Your Thoughts

Once you've read *OpenAI API Cookbook*, we'd love to hear your thoughts! Scan the QR code below to go straight to the Amazon review page for this book and share your feedback.

https://packt.link/r/1805121359

Your review is important to us and the tech community and will help us make sure we're delivering excellent quality content.

Download a free PDF copy of this book

Thanks for purchasing this book!

Do you like to read on the go but are unable to carry your print books everywhere?

Is your eBook purchase not compatible with the device of your choice?

Don't worry, now with every Packt book you get a DRM-free PDF version of that book at no cost.

Read anywhere, any place, on any device. Search, copy, and paste code from your favorite technical books directly into your application.

The perks don't stop there, you can get exclusive access to discounts, newsletters, and great free content in your inbox daily

Follow these simple steps to get the benefits:

1. Scan the QR code or visit the link below

https://packt.link/free-ebook/9781805121350

2. Submit your proof of purchase
3. That's it! We'll send your free PDF and other benefits to your email directly

1
Unlocking OpenAI and Setting Up Your API Playground Environment

ChatGPT, an advanced **artificial intelligence** (**AI**) language model developed by OpenAI, is the fastest-growing original consumer application in history, reaching 100 million users in only 2 months. By comparison, TikTok is in second place, reaching the same number of users in over 9 months (`https://www.forbes.com/sites/cindygordon/2023/02/02/chatgpt-is-the-fastest-growing-ap-in-the-history-of-web-applications/?sh=3551e45d678c`). The reason for its popularity can be attributed to its ability to democratize **Natural Language Processing** (**NLP**) models for the everyday user. NLP represents a domain in AI that focuses on the interaction between computers and humans through natural language. The ultimate goal of NLP is to enable computers to interpret, understand, and respond to human language in a way that is both meaningful and useful. Traditionally, tasks in this field – from sentiment analysis to language translation – required robust datasets and specialized knowledge in machine learning and data science to be effectively executed.

However, the rise of ChatGPT and its associated **Application Programming Interface** (**API**) has revolutionized the NLP landscape. Thanks to its ability to democratize NLP models, anyone, including regular users, can now generate human-like text from prompts without having any in-depth knowledge of data science or machine learning. For instance, whereas previously one might have needed to design a complex model to classify text into categories, with ChatGPT, a simple prompt can often achieve the same goal.

In essence, the advent of ChatGPT has made previously intricate NLP tasks more accessible and user-friendly, bridging the gap between advanced technology and the general public.

Programmers and developers are taking note, integrating GPT's power into their own applications to make them intelligent. In fact, many well-funded start-ups (*Typeface*, *Jasper AI*, *Copy.ai*) have ChatGPT and other **Large Language Models** (**LLMs**) as the basis of their product, whether it's summarizing text, finding information, or creating a chatbot. This requires a fundamental understanding of the OpenAI API and how to use it to build intelligent applications, which is where we'll begin.

This starts with the basics, which involves creating an OpenAI account, accessing the API Playground, and making API requests.

In this chapter, we will cover the following recipes:

- Setting up your OpenAI Playground environment
- Running a completion request in the OpenAI Playground
- Using the System Message in the OpenAI Playground
- Using the Chat Log to modify the model's behavior
- Making OpenAI API requests with Postman

Technical requirements

This chapter requires you to have access to the OpenAI API. You can create an account and register for access at `https://platform.openai.com/overview`.

Setting up your OpenAI Playground environment

The **OpenAI Playground** is an interactive web-based interface designed to allow users to experiment with OpenAI's language models, including ChatGPT. It's a place where you can learn about the capabilities of these models by entering prompts and seeing the responses generated in real time. This platform acts as a sandbox where developers, researchers, and curious individuals alike can experiment, learn, and even prototype their ideas.

In the Playground, you have the freedom to engage in a wide range of activities. You can test out different versions of the AI models, experimenting with various prompts to see how the model responds, and you can play around with different parameters to influence the responses generated. It provides a real-time glimpse into how these powerful AI models think, react, and create based on your input.

Getting ready

Before you start, you need to create an *OpenAI Platform* account.

Navigate to `https://platform.openai.com/` and sign in to your OpenAI account. If you do not have an account, you can sign up for free with an email address. Alternatively, you can log in to OpenAI with a valid Google, Microsoft, or Apple account. Follow the instructions to complete the creation of your account. You may need to verify your identity with a valid phone number.

How to do it...

1. After you have successfully logged in, navigate to **Profile** in the top right-hand menu, select **Personal**, and then select **Usage** from the left-hand side menu. Alternatively, you can navigate to `https://platform.openai.com/account/usage` after logging in. This page shows the usage of your API, but more importantly, it shows you how many credits you have available.

2. Normally, OpenAI provides you a $5 credit with a new account, which you should be able to see under the **Free Trial Usage** section of the page. If you do have credits, proceed to *step 4*. If, however, you do not have any credits, you will need to upgrade and set up a paid account.

3. You need not set up a paid account if you have received free credits. If you run out of free credits, however, here is how you can set up a paid account: select **Billing** from the left-hand side menu and then select **Overview**. Then, select the **Set up paid account** button. You will be prompted to enter your payment details and set a dollar threshold, which can be set to any level of spend that you are comfortable with. Note that the amount of credits required to collectively execute every single recipe contained in this book is not likely to exceed *$5*.

4. After you have created an OpenAI Platform account, you should be able to access the Playground by selecting **Playground** from the top menu bar, or by navigating to `https://platform.openai.com/playground`.

How it works...

The OpenAI Playground interface is, in my experience, clean, intuitive, and designed to provide users easy access to OpenAI's powerful language models. The Playground is an excellent place to learn how the models perform under different settings, allowing you to experiment with parameters such as temperature and max tokens, which influence the randomness and length of the outputs respectively. The changes you make are instantly reflected in the model's responses, offering immediate feedback.

As shown in *Figure 1.1*, the Playground consists of three sections: the *System Message*, the *Chat Log*, and the *Parameters*. You will learn more about these three features in the *Running a completion request in the OpenAI Playground* recipe.

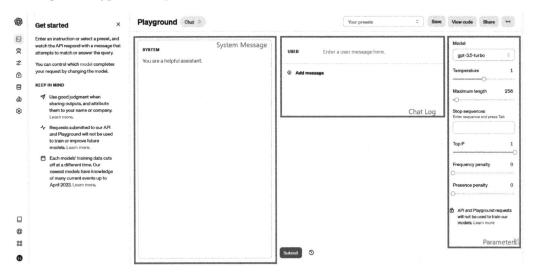

Figure 1.1 – The OpenAI Playground

Now, your Playground is set up and ready to be used. You can use it to run completion requests and see how varying your prompts and parameters affect the response from OpenAI.

Running a completion request in the OpenAI Playground

In this recipe, we will actually put the Playground in action and execute a completion request from OpenAI. Here, you will see the power of the OpenAI API and how it can be used to provide completions for virtually any prompt.

Getting ready

Ensure you have an OpenAI Platform account with available usage credits. If you don't, please follow the *Setting up your OpenAI Playground environment* recipe. All the recipes in this chapter will have this same requirement.

How to do it...

Let's go ahead and start testing the model with the Playground. Let's create an assistant that writes marketing slogans:

1. Navigate to the **OpenAI Playground**.

2. In the System Message, type in the following: You are an assistant that creates marketing slogans based on descriptions of companies. Here, we are clearly instructing the model of its role and context.

3. In the Chat Log, populate the **USER** message with the following: A company that writes engaging mystery novels.

4. Select the **Submit** button on the bottom of the page.

5. You should now see a completion response from OpenAI. In my case (*Figure 1.2*), the response is as follows:

> Unlock the Thrilling Pages of Suspense with Our Captivating Mystery Novels!

Playground   Test   × ∨   Save

SYSTEM
You are an assistant that creates marketing slogans based on descriptions of companies

USER   A company that writes engaging mystery novels

ASSISTANT   "Unlock the Thrilling Pages of Suspense with Our Captivating Mystery Novels!"

⊕ Add message

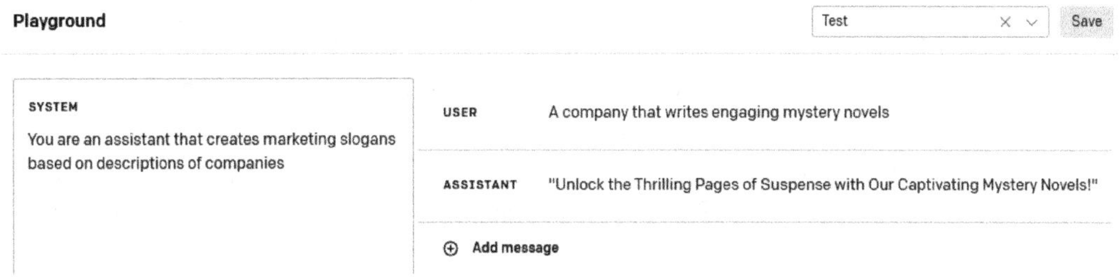

Figure 1.2 – The OpenAI Playground with prompt and completion

> **Note**
> Since OpenAI's LLMs are probabilistic, you will likely not see the same outputs as me. In fact, if you run this recipe multiple times, you will likely see different answers, and that is expected because it is built into the randomness of the model.

How it works...

OpenAI's text generation models utilize a specific neural network architecture termed a transformer. Before delving deeper into this, let's unpack some of these terms:

- **Neural network architecture**: At a high level, this refers to a system inspired by the human brain's interconnected neuron structure. It's designed to recognize patterns and can be thought of as the foundational building block for many modern AI systems.

- **Transformer**: This is a type of neural network design that has proven particularly effective for understanding sequences, making it ideal for tasks involving human language. It focuses on the relationships between words and their context within a sentence or larger text segment.

In machine learning, **unsupervised learning** typically refers to training a model without any labeled data, letting the model figure out patterns on its own. However, OpenAI's methodology is more nuanced. The models are initially trained on a vast corpus of text data, supervised with various tasks. This helps them predict the next word in a sentence, for instance. Subsequent refinements are made using **Reinforcement Learning through Human Feedback** (**RLHF**), where the model is further improved based on feedback from human evaluators.

Through this combination of techniques and an extensive amount of data, the model starts to capture the intricacies of human language, encompassing context, tone, humor, and even sarcasm.

In this case, the completion response is provided based on both the System Message and the Chat Log. The System Message serves a critical role in shaping and guiding the responses you receive from Open AI, as it dictates the model's *persona*, *role*, *tone*, and *context*, among other attributes. In our case, the System Message contains the persona we want the model to take: *You are an assistant that creates marketing slogans based on descriptions of companies.*

The Chat Log contains the history of messages that the model has access to before providing its response, which contains our prompt, `A company that writes engaging mystery novels`.

Finally, the parameters contain more granular settings that you can change for the model, such as temperature. These significantly change the completion response from OpenAI. We will discuss temperature and other parameters in greater detail in *Chapter 3*.

There's more...

It is worth noting that ChatGPT does not read and understand the meaning behind text – instead, the responses are based on statistical probabilities based on patterns it observed during training.

The model does not understand the text in the same way that humans do; instead, the completions are generated based on statistical associations and patterns that have been *trained* in the model's neural network from a large body of similar text. Now, you know how to run completion requests with the OpenAI Playground. You can try this feature out for your own prompts and see what completions you get. Try creative prompts such as `write me a song about lightbulbs` or more professional prompts such as `explain Newton's first law`.

Using the System Message in the OpenAI Playground

In this recipe, we will observe how modifying the System Message affects the completion response that we receive from the model. This is important because as you begin to use the OpenAI API, you will likely adjust and refine the System Message to your specific needs, and the Playground is a great way to try that.

How to do it...

1. Navigate to the OpenAI Playground.

2. In the **SYSTEM** field, type in the following: `You are an assistant that creates engaging and professional company names based on descriptions of companies.`

3. In the Chat Log, populate the **USER** message with the following: `A company that helps you with your taxes.`

4. Select the **Submit** button on the bottom of the page.

5. You should now see a completion response from OpenAI. In my case in *Figure 1.3*, the response is as follows:

    `TaxGuardian.`

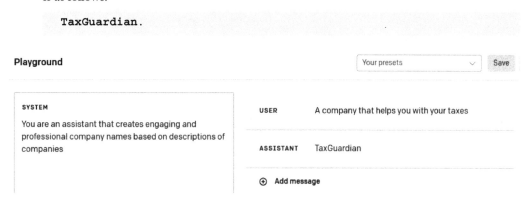

Figure 1.3 – The OpenAI Playground with prompt and completion

6. Hover over the **ASSISTANT** response and select the minus icon on the right-hand side to delete the model's response from the Chat Log. This needs to be done because we want OpenAI to not only generate a response but generate one as the **ASSISTANT**.

7. Modify the System Message to `You are an assistant that creates potential customer segments and marketing strategies based on descriptions of companies.`

8. Select the **Submit** button on the bottom of the page.

9.   You should now see a much longer completion response from OpenAI. In my case, as shown in *Figure 1.4*, the response details potential customer segments:

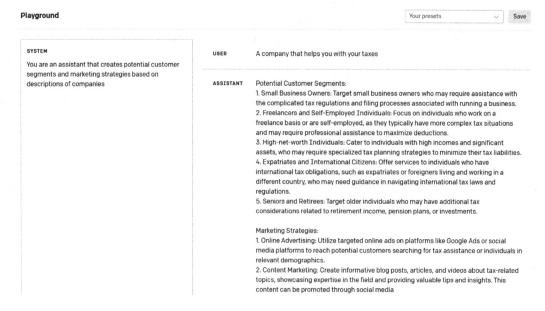

Figure 1.4 – The OpenAI Playground response after modifying the System Message

How it works...

The model generates a completely different type of response after modifying the System Message, even though the prompt in the Chat Log is exactly the same. The response changed from a one-word answer to a multi-paragraph response because of the instructions from the System Message. We also had to remove the default Assistant response because we want OpenAI to generate its own response instead of *feeding* it a response.

The System Message, being the first message in the conversation, heavily influences the *thinking* of the model by providing a frame of reference or context. This context is crucial because, without it, the model would lack necessary guidance to respond appropriately to subsequent user inputs. It is the cornerstone of defining your interaction with the model, allowing you to provide important context and high-level directives that steer the conversation or task at hand.

As a result, when we begin to use the OpenAI API to create business applications, careful considerations must be made to the instructions that we put into the System Message.

There's more...

The beauty of the System Message is that that you can be as simple or as intricate with your instructions as you want. For example, here are common system messages that can be used for various purposes:

- You are an assistant that helps young students learn important concepts in science by explaining concepts in easy-to-understand language

- You are an assistant that creates marketing slogans based on descriptions of companies that are provided to you

- I am planning a birthday party 2 weeks from now for my 5 year old niece and you are my party planner that tells me what I should be doing

Using the Chat Log to modify the model's behavior

In this recipe, we will learn how to modify the Chat Log and how it impacts the completion response that we receive from the model. This is important because developers often find this to be the best way to *fine tune* a model, without actually needing to create a new model. This also follows a *prompt engineering* must-have of providing the model with suitable examples.

How to do it...

We can add examples of prompts and responses to the Chat Log to modify the model's behavior. Let's observe this with the following steps:

1. Navigate to the **OpenAI Playground**. If you already have messages populated, refresh the page to start afresh.

2. In the System Message, type in the following: You are an assistant that creates marketing slogans based on descriptions of companies. Here, we are clearly instructing the model of its role and context.

3. In the Chat Log, populate the **USER** message with the following: A company that makes ice cream.

   Select the **Add message** button located underneath the **USER** label to add a new message. Ensure that the label of the message says **ASSISTANT**. If it does not, select the label to toggle between **USER** and **ASSISTANT**.

   Now, type the following into the **ASSISTANT** message: Sham - the ice cream that never melts!.

4. Select the **Add message** button and ensure that the label of the message says **USER** instead now. Type the following into the **USER** message: `A company that produces comedy movies.`

5. Select the **Add message** button, and ensure that the label of the message says **ASSISTANT**. Type the following into the **ASSISTANT** message: `Sham - the best way to tickle your funny bone!`.

6. Repeat *steps 4-5* once more, with the following **USER** and **ASSISTANT** messages, respectively: `A company that provides legal assistance to businesses, and Sham - we know business law!`. At this point, you should see the following:

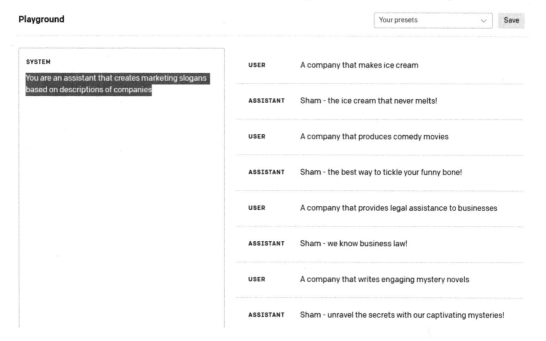

Figure 1.5 – The OpenAI Playground with Chat Logs populated

7. Finally, select the **Add message** button, and create a **USER** message with the following: `A company that writes engaging mystery novels.`

8. Select the **Submit** button on the bottom of the page.

9. You should now see a completion response from OpenAI. In my case (*Figure 1.6*), the response is as follows:

    `Sham - unravel the secrets with our captivating mysteries!`

Yours may be different, but the response you see will definitely start with the word "*Sham –*" and end with an exclamation point. In this way, we have *trained* the model to only give us completion responses in that format.

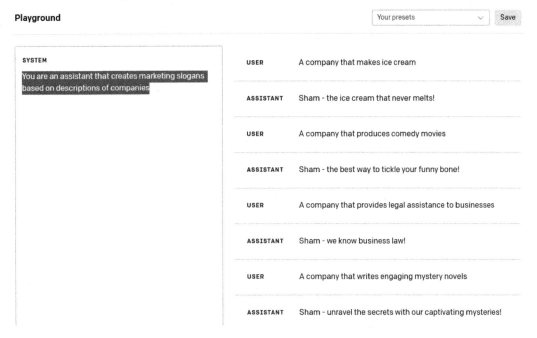

Figure 1.6 – The OpenAI Playground with completion, after changing the Chat Log

How it works...

As we learned in the *Running a completion request in the OpenAI Playground* recipe, ChatGPT and its GPT models are built on a transformer architecture, which processes input and generates responses based on the immediate chat history it has been given. It doesn't have an ongoing memory of past interactions or a stored understanding of context outside the immediate conversation. The Chat Log has a significant impact on the model's completions. When the model receives a prompt, it takes into account the most recent prompt, the System Message, and all the preceding messages in the Chat Log.

We can observe this in the **Playground** by providing our own sets of User and Assistant messages, and then see how the model changes its completion, as we did in the preceding steps.

In particular, the model has detected two patterns in the Chat Log and then generated the completion to follow that behavior:

- The model detected that all manual Assistant completions begin with the word *Sham*, and so it added that prefix to its completion

- The model identified that all slogans end with an exclamation point, and so when it generated the completion, it also added in an exclamation point

Overall, the Chat Log can be used to *train* the model to generate certain types of completions that the user wants to create. In addition, the Chat Log helps the model understand and maintain the context of the bigger conversation.

For example, if you added a User message with `What is an airplane?` and followed it up with another User message of `How do they fly?`, the model would understand that `they` refers to the `airplane` because of the Chat Log.

Prompt engineering

The Chat Log plays a pivotal role in influencing the model's completions, and this observation is a glimpse into the broader realm of **prompt engineering**. Prompt engineering is a technique where the input or **prompt** given to a model is carefully crafted to guide the model towards producing a desired output.

Within the sphere of prompt engineering, there are a few notable concepts, as follows:

- **Zero-shot prompting**: Here, the model is given a task that it hasn't been explicitly trained on. It relies entirely on its pre-existing knowledge and training to generate a relevant response. In essence, it's like asking the model to perform a task *cold*, without any prior examples.

- **Few-shot prompting**: This involves providing the model with a small number of examples related to the desired task. The aim is to nudge the model into recognizing the pattern or context and then generating a relevant completion based on the few examples given.

Understanding these nuances in how prompts can be engineered allows users to leverage ChatGPT's capabilities more effectively, tailoring interactions to their specific needs.

Overall, the Chat Log (and the System Message, as we learned in the earlier recipe) is a great low-touch method of aligning the completion responses from OpenAI to a desired target, without needing to fine-tune the model itself. Now that we've used the Playground to test prompts and completions, it's time to use the actual OpenAI API.

Making OpenAI API requests with Postman

The OpenAI Playground is a great way to test model completions and provides the exact same responses that you would receive with the OpenAI API, but it serves a different purpose. While the Playground is treated as a sandbox for experimentation that is easy to use, interactive, and great for learning, the OpenAI API enables users to integrate the models directly into their applications.

Getting ready

In order to make HTTP requests, we need a client such as Postman to post requests to the API. We also need to generate an **API key**, a unique identifier that authorizes us to make requests to OpenAI's API.

In this recipe and book, we will select Postman as our API client, but note that many alternatives exist, including *WireMock*, *Smartbear*, and *Paw*. We have chosen Postman because it is the most widely used tool, it's cross-platform (meaning that it works on Windows, Mac, and Linux), and finally, for our use case it's completely free.

Installing Postman

Postman is the widely recognized stand-alone tool for testing APIs, used by over 17 million users (`https://blog.postman.com/postman-public-api-network-is-now-the-worlds-largest-public-api-hub/`). It contains many features, but its core use case is enabling developers to send HTTP requests and viewing responses in an easy-to-use user interface. In fact, Postman also contains a web-based version (no downloads necessary), which is what we will be using in this section.

To use Postman, navigate to `https://www.postman.com/` and create a free account using the **Sign Up for Free** button. Follow the on-screen instructions until you get to platform, where you should see a menu bar at the top with options for **Home**, **Workspaces**, **API Network**, and more. Alternatively, you can choose to download and install the Postman application on your computer (follow the steps on the website), removing the need to create a Postman account.

Now that we are on the Postman platform, let's configure our workspace:

1. Select **Workspaces** from the top and click **Create Workspace**.
2. Select **Blank Workspace** and click **Next**.

3.   Give the workspace a name (such as OpenAI API), select **Personal**, and then select **Create**.

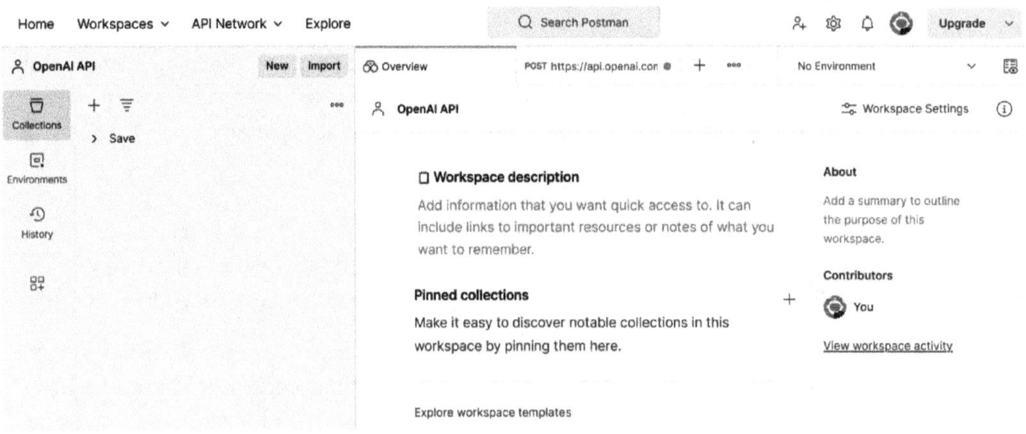

Figure 1.7 – Configuring the Postman workspace

Getting your API key

API keys are used to authenticate HTTP requests to OpenAI's servers. Each API key is unique to an OpenAI Platform account. In order to get your OpenAI API key:

1.   Navigate to `https://platform.openai.com/` and log in to your OpenAI API account.

2.   Select **Personal** from the top right and click **View API keys**.

3.   Select the **Create new secret key** button, type in any name, and then select **Create secret key**.

4.   Your API key should now be visible to you – note it down somewhere safe, such as in a password-protected `.txt` file.

> **Note**
> Your API key is your means of authenticating with OpenAI – it should not be shared with anyone and should be stored as securely as any password.

How to do it...

After setting up our Postman workspace and generating our OpenAI API key, we have everything we need to make HTTP requests to the API. We will first create and send the request, and then analyze the various components of the request.

In order to make an API request using Postman, follow these steps:

1. In your Postman workspace, select the **New** button on the top-left menu bar, and then select **HTTP** from the list of options that appears. This will create a new **Untitled Request**.

2. Change the HTTP request type from **GET** to **POST** in the **Method** drop-down menu (by default, it will be set to **GET**).

3. Enter the following URL as the endpoint for Chat Completions: `https://api.openai.com/v1/chat/completions`

4. Select **Headers** in the sub-menu, and add the following key-value pairs into the table below it:

Key	Value
Content-Type	application/json
Authorization	Bearer <your API key here>

Select **Body** in the sub-menu and then select **raw** for the request type. Enter the following request body, which details to OpenAI the prompt, system message, chat log, and a set of other parameters that it needs to use to generate a completion response:

```
{
   "model": "gpt-3.5-turbo",
   "messages": [
      {
         "role": "system",
         "content": "You are an assistant that creates marketing
slogans based on descriptions of companies"
      },
      {
         "role": "user",
         "content": "A company that writes engaging mystery novels"
      }
   ]
}
```

The **Headers** and **Body** sections of the Postman request should look like this:

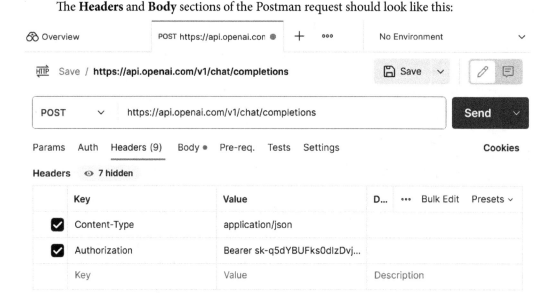

Figure 1.8 – Postman Headers

Figure 1.9 – Postman Body

5. Click the **Send** button on the top right to make your HTTP request.

After sending the HTTP request, you should see the response from OpenAI API. The response is in the form of a **JavaScript Object Notation (JSON)** object.

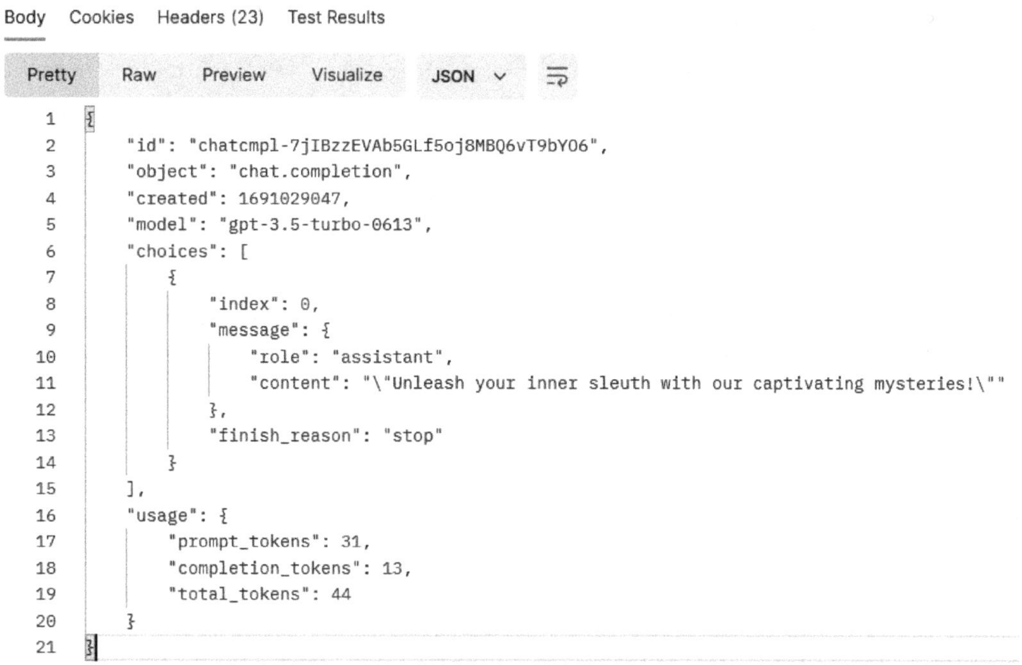

```
Body   Cookies   Headers (23)   Test Results

Pretty    Raw    Preview    Visualize    JSON  ∨    ⇥

 1    {
 2        "id": "chatcmpl-7jIBzzEVAb5GLf5oj8MBQ6vT9bY06",
 3        "object": "chat.completion",
 4        "created": 1691029047,
 5        "model": "gpt-3.5-turbo-0613",
 6        "choices": [
 7            {
 8                "index": 0,
 9                "message": {
10                    "role": "assistant",
11                    "content": "\"Unleash your inner sleuth with our captivating mysteries!\""
12                },
13                "finish_reason": "stop"
14            }
15        ],
16        "usage": {
17            "prompt_tokens": 31,
18            "completion_tokens": 13,
19            "total_tokens": 44
20        }
21    }
```

Figure 1.10 – Postman request body and response

How it works...

In order to build intelligent applications, we need to start using the OpenAI API instead of the Playground. There are other benefits to using the OpenAI API as well, including the following:

- More flexibility, control, and customization of the model, its parameters, and its completions

- Enables you to integrate the power of OpenAI's models directly into your application without your end users interacting with OpenAI at all

- Provides you the power to scale the amount of model requests you're making to fit the load of your application

We are now going to shift our focus exclusively to the API, but seasoned developers will always revert to the Playground to perform testing on their system messages, chat logs, and parameters.

To make API requests, we need two things:

- *A way to make our requests* – For this, we used Postman as it's an easy-to-use tool. When developing applications, however, the app itself will make requests.

- *A way to authenticate our requests* – For this, we generated an API key from our OpenAI account. This tells OpenAI who is making this request.

The actual API request consists of four elements: the *endpoint*, the *Header*, the *body*, and finally, the *response*. Note that this concept is not exclusive to OpenAI but applies to most APIs.

The endpoint

The **endpoint** serves as the location of your HTTP request, which manifests itself in the form of a specific URL. A web server exists at the endpoint URL to listen to requests and provide the corresponding data. With OpenAI, each function corresponds to a different endpoint.

For example, two additional examples of different endpoints within OpenAI are the following:

```
# used for generating images
https://api.openai.com/v1/images/generations
# used for generating embeddings
https://api.openai.com/v1/embeddings
```

Additionally, the OpenAI API endpoint only accepts **POST** method requests. Think of the HTTP methods (POST, GET, etc.) as different ways to travel to a location: by train, air, or sea. In this case, OpenAI only accepts **POST** requests.

The Header

The **Header** of an API request contains metadata about the request itself. Information represented in Header tags contains relevant and important elements about the body, and helps the server interpret the request. Specifically, in our case, we set two Headers:

- `Content-Type`: We set the content-type of our request to `application/json`, meaning that we are telling the server that our request body will be in JSON format.

- `Authorization`: We set the authorization value to the API key, which allows the server to verify the client (Postman and our OpenAI Platform account in our case) that is making the specific request. The server can use the API key to check whether the client has permissions to make the request and whether the client has enough credit available to make the request. It's worth noting that often, API keys are sent as a **Bearer token** within the authorization Header. A Bearer token signifies that the bearer of this token (i.e., the client making the request) is authorized to access specific resources. It serves as a compact and self-contained method for transmitting identity and authorization information between the client and the server.

The Body

Finally, the **Body** of an API request is the request itself, expressed in the JSON notation format (which purposely matches the `Content-Type` defined in the Header of the request). The required parameters for the endpoint that we are using (Chat Completions) are `model` and `messages`:

- `model`: This represents the specific model that is used to produce the completion. In our case, we used `gpt-3.5-turbo`, which represents the latest model that was available at the time. This is equivalent to using the **Model** dropdown in the **Parameters** section of the OpenAI Playground, which we saw in the *Setting up your OpenAI Playground environment* recipe.

- `messages`: This represents the System Message and Chat Log that the model has access to when generating its completion. In a conversation, it represents the list of messages comprising the conversation so far. In JSON, the list is denoted by `[]` to indicate that the message parameter contains a list of JSON objects (messages). Each JSON object (or message) within `messages` must contain a `role` string and a `content` string:

  - `role`: In each message, this represents the role of the message author. To create a System Message, the role should be equal to `system`. To create a User message, the role should be equal to `user`. To create an Assistant message, the role should equal to `assistant`.

  - `content`: This represents the content of the message itself.

In our case, we had set the System Message to `You are an assistant that creates marketing slogans based on descriptions of companies`, and the User message or prompt to `A company that writes engaging mystery novels`. This, in JSON form, is equivalent to our first Playground example.

The response

When we made the preceding request using Postman, we received a **response** from OpenAI in JSON notation. JSON is a lightweight data format that is easy for humans to read and write, and easy for machines to parse and generate. The data format consists of parameters, which are key-value pairs. Each parameter value can be in the form of a string, another JSON object, a list of strings, or a list of JSON objects.

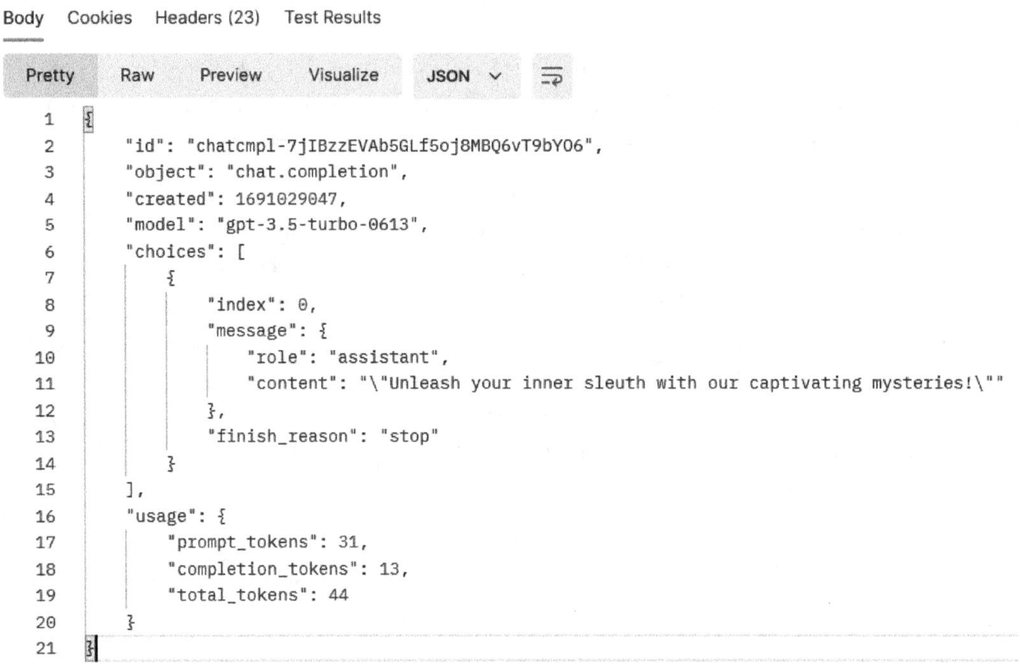

Body   Cookies   Headers (23)   Test Results

| Pretty | Raw | Preview | Visualize | JSON ∨ | ⇥ |

```
1   {
2       "id": "chatcmpl-7jIBzzEVAb5GLf5oj8MBQ6vT9bYO6",
3       "object": "chat.completion",
4       "created": 1691029047,
5       "model": "gpt-3.5-turbo-0613",
6       "choices": [
7           {
8               "index": 0,
9               "message": {
10                  "role": "assistant",
11                  "content": "\"Unleash your inner sleuth with our captivating mysteries!\""
12              },
13              "finish_reason": "stop"
14          }
15      ],
16      "usage": {
17          "prompt_tokens": 31,
18          "completion_tokens": 13,
19          "total_tokens": 44
20      }
21  }
```

Figure 1.11 – Postman OpenAI API response

As you can see in *Figure 1.11*, the response contains both metadata and actual content. The parameters and their meaning are described as follows:

- id: A unique identifier for the transaction – every response has a different ID. This is typically used for record-keeping and tracking purposes.

- object: The designation of the request and object type returned by the API, which in this scenario is chat.completion (as we used the Chat Completions endpoint), signifying the conclusion of a chat request.

- created: A timestamp denoting the exact moment of chat completion creation (based on Unix time)..

- model: The precise model that was used to generate the response, which in this case is gpt-3.5-turbo-0613. Note that this differs from the model parameter in the request body. The model parameter in the **Body** section specifies the model type (gpt-3.5-turbo) that was used, whereas the model parameter in the **Response** section specifies not only the model type, but also the model version (which, in this case, is 0613).

- Choices: An array that comprises the responses generated by the model. Each element of this array contains the following:

  - index: A number that represents the order of the choices, with the first choice having an index of 0

  - message: An object containing the message produced by the assistant, comprising the following:

    - role: The role of the entity generating the message. This is very similar to the roles in the Chat Log within the Playground screen.

    - content: The literal text or output generated by the OpenAI model.

  - finish_reason: A string that indicates why the OpenAI model decided to stop generating further output. In this case, stop means the model concluded the message in a natural way.

- usage: A list of parameters that represent the usage, or costs, of the particular API request:

  - prompt_tokens: The quantity of tokens utilized in the initial prompt or the input message

  - completion_tokens: The number of tokens produced by the model as a response to the prompt

  - total_tokens: An aggregate of the prompt and completion tokens, signifying the total tokens expended for the specific API invocation

The response in JSON format may be difficult for us to read. In fact, what we particularly care about is not id, index, or created, but the content parameter, which contains the response

```
Unleash your inner sleuth with our captivating mysteries!
```

However, the JSON response format is essential when integrating the API into your own applications.

This recipe summarizes the essential elements of the OpenAI API and demonstrates how to use an API client such as Postman to send requests and receive responses. This is important because this is the primary method that we will use to learn more about the API and its various other aspects (such as parameters, different endpoints, interpreting the response, etc.).

2

OpenAI API
Endpoints Explained

The OpenAI API is not just one endpoint, but instead a collection of different endpoints that can be used to generate text completions, images, and even transcribe audio. In this chapter, we dive into all these use cases covering the main endpoints that are used by developers when integrating the OpenAI API into their applications. By the end of this chapter, you will know how to use the diverse capabilities of the OpenAI API, the first step in building intelligent applications. You'll understand the nuances of each endpoint, ensuring that you can tailor your integration to your specific needs. Whether you're aiming to create dynamic text content, generate captivating visuals, or transcribe audio, you will learn how to accomplish these tasks all using the API.

Specifically, we will cover the following recipes in this chapter:

- Generating customized responses using the Chat Completions endpoint
- Creating pictures using the Images endpoint
- Generating transcripts using the Audio endpoint

Technical requirements

This chapter requires you to have access to the OpenAI API (via a generated API key) and have an API client installed, such as Postman. You can refer to the *Making OpenAI API requests with Postman* recipe in *Chapter 1* for more information on how to obtain your API key and set up Postman.

Generating customized responses using the Chat Completions endpoint

We previously explored the Chat Completions endpoint at the end of *Chapter 1*, but our request body was fairly simple and did not make use of the important parameters that we also discussed in the *Running a completion request in the OpenAI Playground* recipe. For example, we learned how the Chat Log could be used to *fine-tune* the responses that are generated. Additionally, the Chat Log feature can be used to deploy a chat bot inside your application.

In this recipe, we will cover how to generate responses using the Chat Completions endpoint while using the Chat Log parameters.

Getting ready

Ensure you have an OpenAI Platform account with available usage credits. If you don't, please follow the *Setting up your OpenAI Playground environment* recipe in *Chapter 1*.

Furthermore, ensure you have Postman installed, you have created a new workspace, you have created a new HTTP request, and that the `Headers` for that request are correctly configured. This is important because without the `Authorization` configured, you will not be able to use the API. If you don't have Postman installed and configured as mentioned, please follow the *Making OpenAI API requests with Postman* recipe in *Chapter 1*.

All the recipes in this chapter will have this same requirement.

How to do it...

1. In Postman, create a new request by selecting the **New** button on the top-left menu bar, and then select **HTTP**.

2. Change the HTTP request type from **GET** to **POST** in the **Method** drop-down menu (by default, it will be set to **GET**).

3. Enter the following URL as the endpoint for Chat Completions: `https://api.openai.com/v1/chat/completions`.

4. Select **Headers** from the sub-menu and add the following key-value pairs into the table below it:

Key	Value
Content-Type	application/json
Authorization	Bearer <your API key here>

Select **Body** from the sub-menu and then select **raw** for the request type. Enter the following in **Body**. After that, select **Send**:

```
{
    "model": "gpt-3.5-turbo",
    "messages": [
        {
            "role": "system",
            "content": "You are an assistant that creates short
one-line responses to comments that users have left on your ice
cream shop's Google reviews page"
        },
        {
            "role": "user",
            "content": "Comments: Great experience - I love the
vanilla flavor!"
        }
    ]
}
```

5. After sending the HTTP request, you should see the following response from the OpenAI API. Note that your response may be different. The section of the HTTP response that we particularly want to take note of is the content value:

```
{
    "id": "chatcmpl-710Y7gmS2gtyxyvX7VaSCKiU2oHgB",
    "object": "chat.completion",
    "created": 1691437883,
    "model": "gpt-3.5-turbo-0613",
    "choices": [
        {
            "index": 0,
            "message": {
                "role": "assistant",
                "content": "Thank you for your kind words!
Vanilla is always a classic favorite. 😊🍦"
            },
            "finish_reason": "stop"
        }
    ],
    "usage": {
        "prompt_tokens": 47,
        "completion_tokens": 19,
        "total_tokens": 66
    }
}
```

6. Let's now add messages into the Chat Log (or `messages`, as it's referred to in the API) to modify and tune the responses that are generated. Modify **Body** to the following – take note of the highlighted sections, where we have added chats to the list inside `messages`:

```
{
  "model": "gpt-3.5-turbo",
  "messages": [
    {
      "role": "system",
      "content": "You are an assistant that creates short
one-line responses to comments that users have left on your ice
cream shop's Google reviews page"
    },
    {
      "role": "user",
      "content": "Comments: Great experience - I love the
vanilla flavor!"
    },
    {
      "role": "assistant",
      "content": "Hello Ice Cream Fan, thank you so much.
Vanilla is our favorite too. SCREAM FOR ICE CREAM!"
    },
    {
      "role": "user",
      "content": "Comments: I liked the many different flavors
they have, and there's no line!"
    },
    {
      "role": "assistant",
      "content": "Hello Ice Cream Fan, thanks for that - we have
over 50 different flavors. SCREAM FOR ICE CREAM!"
    },
    {
      "role": "user",
      "content": "Comments: The customer service was great -
they were all so helpful!"
    },
    {
      "role": "assistant",
      "content": "Hello Ice Cream Fan, much appreciated. So glad
we were helpful. SCREAM FOR ICE CREAM!"
    },
    {
```

```
        "role": "user",
        "content": "Comments: great location and great staff"
    }
   ]
}
```

7. Click **Send** to execute the HTTP request. You should see a response similar to the following from the OpenAI API:

```
{
    "id": "chatcmpl-7l0vHiJlRrMrrWhjeJhBMEnT1HyHD",
    "object": "chat.completion",
    "created": 1691439319,
    "model": "gpt-3.5-turbo-0613",
    "choices": [
        {
            "index": 0,
            "message": {
                "role": "assistant",
                "content": "Hello Ice Cream Fan, thank you for
the kind words. We love our location and our staff too. SCREAM
FOR ICE CREAM!"
            },
            "finish_reason": "stop"
        }
    ],
    "usage": {
        "prompt_tokens": 177,
        "completion_tokens": 28,
        "total_tokens": 205
    }
}
```

How it works...

The OpenAI API works very similar to the **Playground**, where developers can add messages to the *Chat Log*. This, in turn, fine-tunes the responses that the API generates – it learns from the assistant responses that we have created.

We did this by first executing a simple chat completion request, and only specified a System message and a User message (i.e., the prompt), as shown in *Figure 2.1*.

```
        "model": "gpt-3.5-turbo",
        "messages": [
          {
System      "role": "system",
message      "content": "You are an assistant that creates short one-line responses to comments that
            users have left on your ice cream shop's Google reviews page"
          },
User      {
message      "role": "user",
            "content": "Comments: Great experience - I love the vanilla flavour!"
          }
Assistant   {
message      "role": "assistant",
            "content": "Hello Ice Cream Fan, thank you so much. Vanilla is our favourite too. SCREAM
            FOR ICE CREAM!"
          },
User      {
message      "role": "user",
            "content": "Comments: I liked the many different flavours they have, and there's no line!"
          },
Assistant   {
message      "role": "assistant",
            "content": "Hello Ice Cream Fan, thanks for that - we have over 50 different flavours.
            SCREAM FOR ICE CREAM!"
          },
User      {
message      "role": "user",
            "content": "Comments: The customer service was great - they were all so helpful!"
          },
Assistant   {
message      "role": "assistant",
            "content": "Hello Ice Cream Fan, much appreciated. So glad we were helpful. SCREAM FOR
            ICE CREAM!"
          },
User      {
message      "role": "user",
(prompt)     "content": "Comments: great location and great staff"
          }
```

Figure 2.1 – Excerpt of messages object within the request body

This was done by adding message objects within the messages object in **Body**. Each message object must contain a *role* and some *content*, as we learned in *Chapter 1*.

We can then add additional Assistant and User messages to teach the model how it should formulate its responses. Importantly, the model will attempt to match any pattern it sees within the messages tagged as Assistant. It is almost as if we are *teaching* the model how it should generate its responses. In this case, all of the Assistant responses contained the words `Hello Ice Cream Fan` and `SCREAM FOR ICE CREAM!`

As a result of us adding messages to the *Chat Log*, when we provided the API with an additional prompt, it returned a response that matched the pattern described in the preceding paragraph:

`Hello Ice Cream Fan, thank you for the kind words. We love our location and our staff too. SCREAM FOR ICE CREAM!`

In this recipe, we learned how to use the Chat Completions endpoint in the OpenAI API to generate text, and how to use the System Message, User prompts, and Chat Log to modify the generated text. This is important because the Chat Completions endpoint is the most common OpenAI API endpoint to use when integrating with other systems to create intelligent applications. Furthermore, as we begin to load the API for practical purposes, it's important to know how to adjust the generated text to fit our desired use case using levers such as the Chat Log.

There's more...

Adding messages to the *Chat Log* has many more purposes than just fine-tuning the assistant responses. Another important use case is creating a chat bot, where the conversation (the preceding User and Assistant messages) must be taken into context before a response can be generated. For instance, consider the following example:

```
System: You are an AI assistant that answers questions about the solar
system
User: What's the largest planet in our solar system?
Assistant: The largest planet in the solar system is Jupiter
User: How big is it?
```

Note that the preceding block is pseudocode for the purposes of illustration and because it's easier to read than the proper JSON structure that would be required for the OpenAI API. In order to use this example in the OpenAI API, the request **Body** would need to be what is displayed in the following code block:

```
{
   "model": "gpt-3.5-turbo",
   "messages": [
      {
         "role": "system",
         "content": " You are an AI assistant that answers questions
about the solar system"
      },
      {
         "role": "user",
         "content": "What's the largest planet in our solar system?"
      },
      {
         "role": "assistant",
         "content": "The largest planet in the solar system is Jupiter"
      },
      {
         "role": "user",
         "content": "How big is it?"
```

```
        }
    ]
}
```

Here, the user prompt is `How big is it?`. However, if we were to call the API using just this prompt, it would not generate the correct answer – in fact, it wouldn't know at all what we were talking about because the previous `User` and `Assistant` messages are not in the request **Body**.

As a result, we would need to construct the request body with all of the messages listed in the preceding code block for the model to provide an accurate response.

Creating pictures using the Images endpoint

The OpenAI API can do more than generate text (although that is its main purpose); it can also create images. It does this with a similar methodology to text generation, but instead of predicting characters, it predicts pixels. The inner workings of the model are complex (it involves the use of encoders, decoders, and embeddings), but that doesn't stop us from actually using the model.

This significantly opens up the types of applications you can create with the OpenAI API. For example, you can create an application that produces stock images based on a user prompt. In this recipe, we will use the OpenAI API to generate several types of images.

How to do it...

1. In Postman, create a new request by selecting the **New** button on the top-left menu bar, and then select **HTTP**.

2. Change the HTTP request type from **GET** to **POST** in the **Method** drop-down menu (by default, it will be set to **GET**).

3. Enter the following URL as the endpoint for images: `https://api.openai.com/v1/images/generations`

4. Select **Headers** in the sub-menu, and add the following key-value pairs into the table below it:

Key	Value
Content-Type	application/json
Authorization	Bearer <your API key here>

Select **Body** in the sub-menu and then select **raw** for the request type. Enter the following and after that, select **Send**:

```
{
    "prompt": "A dog",
    "n": 1,
    "size": "1024x1024"
}
```

5. After sending the HTTP request, you should see the following response from the OpenAI API. Note that your response will be different – it will produce a completely different URL. The following URL has been artificially condensed:

```
{
    "created": 1691525818,
    "data": [
        {
            "url": "https://oaidalleapiprodscus.blob.core.
windows.net/private/org-SdhfpAqxiHTuyKDLiHYAve6V/user-
6A9i4gNyfxN9e9i2e0IUqomI/img-[...]%3D"
        }
    ]
}
```

6. The image is contained within the URL that is generated in the response. Copy the URL from the `url` object and paste it into your internet browser. You should see an image of a dog. Similar to text generation, the image that you see will be different than the following one.

Figure 2.2 – Output of DALLE-2 OpenAI image generation of a dog

7. Return to Postman and modify the request **Body**. Change the prompt object to the following phrase and then select **Send**: `A brown furry medium-sized corgi dog on a green grass field, profile view.`

8. Copy and paste the URL from the **Response** field into your browser, and should see a clear photo of a Corgi dog.

Figure 2.3 – Output of DALL-E 2 OpenAI image generation with a more detailed prompt

How it works...

The Images endpoint works using an AI model called **DALL-E**, which is a variation of the GPT model, but used to produce visualizations instead of text output. The model was trained on several billion image-text prompts to associate certain textual characteristics with visual representations. The power of this model is available within OpenAI, but a particular endpoint needs to be used, as we described in the recipe.

> **Note**
>
> DALL-E was introduced by OpenAI in early 2021 as its first text-to-image generation model. DALL-E 2, its next iteration, was released one year later (`https://openai.com/dall-e-2`).
>
> Both DALL-E and DALL-E 2 serve the same purpose (generating images from text) and are even called using the same API. The key difference is that DALL-E 2 employs a more advanced and more popular technique called **diffusion**, a particular image generation method that leads to more realistic and high-resolution images.
>
> In this book, DALL-E and DALL-E 2 will be used interchangeably to refer to the OpenAI's text-to-image generation model.

Request body and response

The request **Body** for the Images endpoint is actually far simpler than the Chat Completions endpoint. Here are all its components:

- prompt: This is the textual instruction provided to the model for image generation. Usually, the more detailed this statement is, the more accurate your desired image will be.

- n: This expresses to the API the number of images that the model should generate. Each image will have slightly different variations, as the model attempts to provide different interpretations or angles based on the prompt.

- size: This specifies the dimensions of the generated image. Note that, at this point, only the following image sizes can be created: 256x256, 512x512, and 1024x1024.

The **Response** that we receive from the Images endpoint is also very easy to understand:

- created: This represents the Unix timestamp of when the image was generated

- data: The value of this object is actually an array of objects, each containing the url parameter:

  - url: This contains the direct link to the generated image

Importance of being detailed

Unlike text generation, where you can afford to be a bit general and any ambiguity is usually addressed by the context of the Chat Log and System Message, image generation requires detailed, descriptive, and specific language to produced the desired output. We clearly saw this in this recipe. The simle prompt, A dog, resulted in a standard image of a dog, but observe in *Figure 2.4* the variation of images that are produced when we run image generation again with the same prompt.

Figure 2.4 – Outputs generated for the same image prompt

The images contain different types of dogs, different environments, different angles, and different lighting. Compare this to the more detailed prompt we used – the following figure shows the additional images that were produced by the more detailed prompt about a Corgi in this recipe.

Figure 2.5 – Different outputs generated from a specific prompt

A more descriptive prompt significantly narrows down the possibilities, guiding the model towards producing an image that matches the user's wants and intentions. It's important to specify colors, positioning, objects, emotions, lighting, and other details so that the user can ensure that the generated image is not only relevant but also intricately tailored to their requirements.

The Images endpoint in the OpenAI API unlocks a variety of different use cases. For example, the endpoint can be used to build personalized pictures in stories, visualize different food recipe ideas, and even create funny pictures for greeting cards. The possibilities are truly endless!

Generating transcripts using the Audio endpoint

In this recipe, we will learn how to use the OpenAI API's Audio endpoint, which converts audio into text. This enables developers to create voice applications, such as voice agents and speech conversational bots.

Getting ready

This recipe will also use Postman, but the typical set of Headers that we use will need to be modified so that the HTTP client uses form data instead of typical JSON. In addition, we must have a sample audio file that we can use as an example to convert speech to text. **Form data** is a way to encode and send data as key-value pairs in HTTP requests instead of JSON-formatted strings. Form data is often used for uploading files.

After opening a new request in Postman, navigate to the **Headers** menu and delete the `Content-Type application/json` entry. This will force Postman to default to the `Content-Type` of the request based on what is passed in the request **Body**.

Next, we need an audio file. Any short (i.e., less than a minute) file will do, but it must contain words that can be transcribed and must be in one of the following formats: `.mp3`, `.mp4`, `.mpeg`, `.mpga`, `.m4a`, `.wav`, or `.webm`. You can also download a 10-second audio snip that I created here: `https://github.com/hasygithub/ChatGPT-API-Book/raw/main/audiosample.mp3`.

How to do it...

We can add examples of prompts and responses to the Chat Log to modify the model's behavior. Let's observe this with the following steps:

1. In Postman, change the **Endpoint** value to the following URL and change the request type to **Post**:

    `https://api.openai.com/v1/audio/transcriptions`

2. Select **Body**, and then select the **form-data** radio button. This will open the form data fields. Each field contains a **Key** and a **Value**.

> **Note**
>
> We have the option to set each field as **Text** or **File**. We can do this by hovering over **Key** and selecting our chosen option from the drop-down menu, as demonstrated in *Figure 2.6*.

3. Enter the following fields in the form data:

Key	Instruction/Value
file	Click **Select Files** and upload the audio file you created or downloaded earlier
model	whisper-1

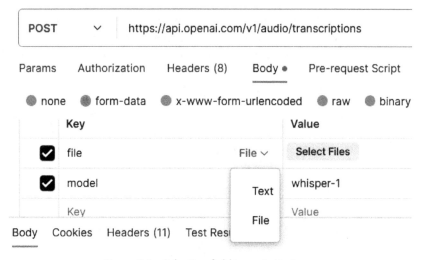

Figure 2.6 – Selecting field types in Postman

4. Select the **Send** button to submit the HTTP request.

5. You should see the following response from OpenAI, specifying the text that was transcribed:

```
{
"text": "This is a test of the Whisper model."
}
```

How it works...

This recipe uses the *Audio* endpoint, but note that the way we interacted with this endpoint's API was completely different than the other endpoints. In particular, this endpoint expects the `Content-Type` of the request to be `form-data`, instead of the typical JSON structure that we saw previously. The reason for this is because `form-data` is capable of handling file streaming, which we needed here as we are uploading audio to OpenAI. In the other endpoints, raw JSON is sufficient because only text is being sent to OpenAI, not files.

HTTP requests are the bedrock of data communication on the web and are frequently used to interact with APIs. Two options for sending data within HTTP requests are **JSON** and **forms**. JSON has now become the ubiquitous data interchange format due to its flexibility in structure – it can be used to communicate key-value pairs, lists, and hierarchy concepts. However, the reason we used forms is that they enable developers to encode binary data. In short, forms enable you to transfer files (such as a 10-second MP3 file, in this case).

In the form, there were two fields: **file** and **model**. The **file** field represents the audio file object that we want to transcribe, and the **model** field represents the particular transcription model we want to use – which, in this case, was actually limited to only one option: **whisper-1**.

The **Response** is simple – a JSON with one object (*text*), representing the transcribed text.

Now that we know how to use this endpoint, we can integrate it to create powerful and smart business applications. For example, typical workflows such as transcribing recorded meetings and lectures can be done with a single API request. Several endpoints can be chained together for even more advanced use cases. For example, we can create voice assistants similar to Siri that take a recorded voice, convert it to text, and then call the Chat Completions API to get a response.

It's important to know that the OpenAI API is more than just text generation; it can perform image generation, voice-to-text, and even create embeddings for semantic search. The OpenAI API is a collection of several different endpoints that, when combined, offer developers an invaluable set of tools to build intelligent applications.

3

Understanding Key Parameters and Their Impact on Generated Responses

In the previous chapter, we learned that the OpenAI API is not just one endpoint but also a collection of various endpoints. These endpoints are triggered with **HTTP** requests, which contain parameters in the corresponding request **Body**. For chat completions, the two required parameters are `model` and `messages` – and we've mainly seen how changing the messages parameter impacts the generated response. However, there is a vast collection of optional parameters that influence the behavior of the API, such as temperature, N, and the maximum number of tokens.

In this chapter, we will explore these optional key parameters and understand how they influence the generated response. **Parameters** are like the dials and knobs you'd find on a complex machine. By adjusting these dials and knobs, you can change the behavior of the machine to your liking. Similarly, in the realm of ChatGPT, parameters allow us to tweak the finer details of the model's behavior, influencing how it processes input and crafts its output. Each of these plays a unique role in shaping the response from OpenAI.

By the end of this chapter, you will know how these parameters can be adjusted to better suit your specific needs, how they affect the quality, length, and style of the output, and how to make effective use of them to get the most desirable results. Learning this is important, as these parameters will need to change as we begin integrating the API for different use cases in intelligent applications, and understanding how generated responses change with these parameters will enable us to determine the correct settings.

Specifically, we will cover the following recipes, each of which will focus on a key parameter:

- Changing the model parameter and understanding its impact on generated responses
- Controlling the number of generated responses using the n parameter
- Determining the randomness and creativity of generated responses using the temperature parameter

Technical requirements

All the recipes in this chapter require you to have access to the OpenAI API (via a generated API key) and have an API client installed, such as Postman. You can refer to the *Chapter 1* recipe *Making OpenAI API requests with Postman* for more information on how to obtain your API key and set up Postman.

Changing the model parameter and understanding its impact on generated responses

In both *Chapter 1* and *Chapter 2*, the chat completion requests were made using both the model and messages parameters, with model always being equal to the gpt-3.5-turbo value. We essentially ignored the model parameter. However, this parameter likely has the biggest impact on the generated responses of any other parameter. Contrary to popular belief, the OpenAI API is not just one model; it's powered by a diverse set of models with different capabilities and price points.

In this recipe, we will cover two main models (*GPT-3.5* and *GPT-4*), learn how to change the model parameter, and observe how the generated responses vary between these two models.

Getting ready

Ensure you have an OpenAI Platform account with available usage credits. If you don't, please follow the *Setting up your OpenAI Playground environment* recipe in *Chapter 1*.

Furthermore, ensure that you have Postman installed, that you have created a new workspace, that you have created a new HTTP request, and that Headers for that request are correctly configured. This is important because, without the Authorization configured, you will not be able to use the API. If you don't have Postman installed and configured as mentioned, follow the *Making OpenAI API requests with Postman* recipe in *Chapter 1*. However, if you do not remember, *steps 1–4* in the next section explain the configuration process.

All the recipes in this chapter will have this same requirement.

How to do it...

1. In your Postman workspace, select the **New** button on the top-left menu bar, and then select **HTTP** from the list of options that appears. This will create a new **Untitled Request**.

2. Change the HTTP request type from **GET** to **POST** by selecting the **Method** drop-down menu (by default, it will be set to **GET**).

3. Enter the following URL as the endpoint for chat completions: `https://api.openai.com/v1/chat/completions`.

4. Select **Headers** in the sub-menu, and add the following key-value pairs into the table below it:

Key	Value
Content-Type	application/json
Authorization	Bearer <your API key here>

Select **Body** in the sub-menu, and then select **raw** for the request type. Enter the following request body, which details to OpenAI the prompt, system message, chat log, and the set of other parameters that it needs to use to generate a completion response:

```
{
    "model": "gpt-3.5-turbo",
    "messages": [
        {
            "role": "user",
            "content": "Describe Donald Trump's time in office in a
    sentence that has six five-letter words. Remember, each word
    must have 5 letters"
        }
    ]
}
```

5. After sending the HTTP request, you should see the following response from the OpenAI API. Note that your response may be different. The section of the HTTP response that we particularly want to take note of is the `content` value:

```
{
    "id": "chatcmpl-7rocZGT1K0edeqZ2dTx65sfWIGdQm",
    "object": "chat.completion",
    "created": 1693060327,
    "model": "gpt-3.5-turbo-0613",
    "choices": [
        {
            "index": 0,
            "message": {
                "role": "assistant",
                "content": "Donald Trump's presidency showcased
```

```
divisive politics and tumultuous events."
            },
            "finish_reason": "stop"
        }
    ],
    "usage": {
        "prompt_tokens": 33,
        "completion_tokens": 12,
        "total_tokens": 45
    }
}
```

6. Let's now repeat the HTTP request in *step 4* and keep everything else consistent, but modify the `model` parameter. Specifically, we will change the value of that parameter to `gpt-4`. Enter the following for the endpoint and request body, and then click **Send**:

```
{
    "model": "gpt-4",
    "messages": [
        {
            "role": "user",
            "content": "Describe Donald Trump's time in office in a
sentence that has six five-letter words. Remember, each word
must have 5 letters"
        }
    ]
}
```

7. You should see the following similar response from the OpenAI API. Note that the response is far different than what we received earlier. Notably, it more closely matches the instruction in the prompt of generating six five-letter words:

```
# Response
{
    "id": "chatcmpl-7rohvZHiQHG0GPh0Ii0Qlcukdk8k7",
    "object": "chat.completion",
    "created": 1693060659,
    "model": "gpt-4",
    "choices": [
        {
            "index": 0,
            "message": {
                "role": "assistant",
                "content": "Trump faced query, shook norms,
split base"
```

```
            },
            "finish_reason": "stop"
        }
    ],
    "usage": {
        "prompt_tokens": 33,
        "completion_tokens": 8,
        "total_tokens": 38
    }
}
```

8. Repeat *steps 1–4*, but change the `content` parameter inside `messages` to the following
    prompt instead: How many chemicals exist in cigarettes, how many of
    them are known to be harmful, and how many are known to cause
    cancer? Respond with just the numbers, nothing else.

    Again, execute one chat completion request where the `model` parameter is gpt-3.5-turbo
    and one where the `model` parameter is gpt-4.

9. The following are extracts of the HTTP response that I received using GPT-3.5-turbo and GPT-4:

    - When model = gpt-3.5-turbo:

    ```
    "content": "There are thousands of chemicals in cigarettes, more
    than 7,000. Over 70 of them are known to be harmful, and at
    least 69 are known to cause cancer."
    ```

    - When model = gpt-4:

    ```
    "content": "6000, 250, 60"
    ```

10. Repeat *steps 4–7*, but change the `content` parameter inside `messages` to the following
    logical question prompt instead:

    ```
    {
      "model": "gpt-3.5-turbo",
      "messages": [
        {
          "role": "user",
          "content": "Which conclusion follows from the statement
    with absolute certainty?\n1. None of the stamp collectors is an
    architect.\n2. All the drones are stamp collectors.\nOptions:\
    na) All stamp collectors are architects.\nb) Architects are not
    drones.\nc) No stamp collectors are drones.\nd) Some drones are
    architects.\nOnly reply with the answer"
        }
      ]
    }
    ```

Note that HTTP requests, with the request body being in the JSON format, cannot handle multiline strings. As a result, if you need to write multiline strings into any of the API parameters (such as `messages` in this case), use the line break characters instead (`\n`):

For example,

```
"
    Line 1
    Line 2
"
```

would become

```
"Line 1\nLine 2"
```

11. The following are extracts of the HTTP response that I received:

    - When `model` = `gpt-3.5-turbo`:

      ```
      "content": "c) No stamp collectors are drones."
      ```

    - When `model` = `gpt-4`:

      ```
      "content": "b) Architects are not drones."
      ```

How it works...

In this recipe, we observed three different examples of how changing the `model` parameter affected the generated text. The following table summarizes the different responses generated by OpenAI, based on different model parameters:

Prompt	Response when model = gpt-3.5-turbo	Response when model = gpt-4
Describe Donald Trump's time in office in a sentence that has six five-letter words. Remember, each word must have five letters	`Donald Trump's presidency showcased divisive politics and tumultuous events.`	`Trump faced query, shook norms, split base`
How many chemicals exist in cigarettes, how many of them are known to be harmful, and how many are known to cause cancer? Respond with just the numbers, nothing else	`There are thousands of chemicals in cigarettes, more than 7,000. Over 70 of them are known to be harmful, and at least 69 are known to cause cancer.`	`6000, 250, 60`

Prompt	Response when model = gpt-3.5-turbo	Response when model = gpt-4
Which conclusion follows from the statement with absolute certainty? 1. None of the stamp collectors is an architect. 2. All the drones are stamp collectors.	```c) No stamp collectors are drones.```	```b) Architects are not drones.```

In all cases, the gpt-4 model produced more accurate results than gpt-3.5-turbo. For example, in the first prompt about describing *Donald Trump's time in office*, the gpt-3.5-turbo model did not understand that it should only use five-letter words, whereas gpt-4 was able to answer it successfully.

GPT-4 versus GPT-3.5

Why is that the case? The inner workings of the two models are different. In neural network models such as GPT, a parameter is a single numerical value that combines with others, which perform calculations that turn inputs (such as a prompt) into output data (such as a chat completion response). The larger the number of parameters, the greater the capacity for the model to accurately capture patterns in the data.

The GPT-3.5 set of models was trained with 175 billion parameters, whereas the GPT-4 set of models is estimated to be trained on more than 100 trillion parameters (collectively over an ensemble of smaller models), many order of magnitudes higher (https://www.pcmag.com/news/the-new-chatgpt-what-you-get-with-gpt-4-vs-gpt-35). The neural network behind GPT-4 is far denser, enabling it to understand nuances and answer more accurately.

GPT models typically struggle with very complex and long instructions. For example, in the cigarette question, the instruction was clearly to respond with just the numbers, nothing else. GPT-3.5 provided a suitable answer, but not in the correct format, whereas the answer returned by GPT-4 was in the correct format.

In general, GPT-4 is more reliable and can handle much more nuanced instructions than GPT-3.5. It is worth noting that the distinction can be subtle, even non-existent, for primarily easy tasks. To discern these differences, the two models were tested on a variety of benchmarks and common exams, which demonstrates the power of GPT-4. You can learn about these test results here: https://openai.com/research/gpt-4. Overall, GPT-4 outperformed GPT-3.5 on various standardized exams, such as AP calculus, AP English literature, and LSAT.

Other differences between GPT-4 and GPT-3.5 include the following:

- **Memory and context size**: GPT-4 can retain more memory and has a bigger context window (`https://platform.openai.com/docs/models`), which means it can accept much larger and more complex prompts than GPT-3.5. The **context window** refers to the amount of recent input (in terms of tokens or chunks of text) the model can consider when generating a response. Imagine reading a paragraph from the middle of a book; the more sentences you can see and remember, the better you understand that paragraph's context. Similarly, with a larger context window, GPT-4 can *see* and *remember* more of the previous input, allowing it to generate more contextually relevant responses.

- **Visual input**: GPT-4 can accept both text and images, whereas GPT-3.5 is text-only.

- **Language**: Both GPT-3.5 and GPT-4 have multilingual capabilities, meaning they can understand, interpret, and respond in languages other than English. However, while GPT-3.5 can work in multiple languages, GPT-4 offers enhanced linguistic finesse and can go beyond simple speech in other languages.

- **Alignment**: GPT-4 has been more *aligned*, meaning it has a bias to not provide harmful advice, buggy code, or inaccurate information, from human-based adversarial testing. In this context, **alignment** refers to the process of adjusting GPT-4's responses to be more in line with ethical and safety standards, reducing the likelihood of it providing harmful advice, buggy code, or inaccurate information.

Cost considerations

One important difference between GPT-4 and GPT-3.5 is cost. GPT-4 charges a much higher token rate, which also increases if models with larger context windows are chosen.

A **token** is a chunk of text that the model reads as input or generates as output. These tokens may be a single character, part of a word, or the word itself. As a rough rule of thumb, 1 token is equal to 0.75 words (`https://platform.openai.com/docs/introduction/key-concepts`).

When making API requests for chat completions, the response always includes the number of tokens that was used in the request, in the `usage` object. For example, the following is an excerpt for the response in *step 5*:

```
"usage": {
        "prompt_tokens": 33,
        "completion_tokens": 12,
        "total_tokens": 45
    }
```

This tells us that our `Describe Donald Trump's time in office in a sentence that has six five-letter words. Remember, each word must have 5 letters` prompt was 33 tokens, and the following response was 12 tokens, making a combined total of 45 tokens:

> **Donald Trump's presidency showcased divisive politics and tumultuous events**

The number of tokens matters for two reasons:

- Depending on the model chosen, the number of total tokens cannot exceed the model's *max token*, also known as the context window. For GPT-3.5-turbo, this is 4,096 tokens. This means that in any API request using that model, the sum of *content* in `messages` cannot exceed 4,096 tokens, or approximately 3,000 words. In comparison, GPT-4 has a sub-model called `gpt-4-32k`, which has a context window of 32,768 tokens, or around 24,000 words.

- The number of total tokens and the model you use dictates how much you are charged for an API request. For example, in *step 5*, we used 45 tokens using the `gpt-3.5-turbo` model, which means that the request cost USD 0.0000675. By comparison, the same 45 tokens using `gpt-4` would have cost USD 0.00135, which is 20x the cost.

Decision criteria

The determination of which model to use in chat completion requests should depend on the following factors:

- **Context window**: Determine the likely context window of the chat completion requests. If your prompts are likely to be over 12,000 words, then you need to use GPT-4, as the biggest model underneath GPT-3.5 only has a maximum number of 16,384 tokens.

- **Complexity**: Determine the complexity of your chat completion request. In general, if it requires nuance understanding and formatting instructions such as the first two examples in the recipe, or if it requires complex information synthesis and logical problem solving such as the third example in the recipe, then you need to use GPT-4. This is especially the case with any mathematical or scientific reasoning – GPT-4 performs far better.

- **Cost**: Evaluate the cost implications of choosing GPT-4 over GPT-3.5. If you use the GPT-4 model with the highest context window, this can be 40x times the price of a request using GPT-3.5.

In general, you should always use and test GPT-3.5 first to see whether it can provide suitable chat completions, and then move to GPT-4 if absolutely necessary.

Overall, the `model` parameter influences the quality of generated responses, which is important, as different use cases of API requests will require different levels of sophisticated responses.

Controlling the number of generated responses using the n parameter

For certain intelligent applications that you build, you want multiple generated texts from the same prompt. For example, if we're building an app that generates company slogans, you likely want to generate not just one but also multiple responses so that the user can select the best one. The n parameter controls how many chat completion choices to generate for each input message. It can also control the number of images that are generated when using the *Images* endpoint.

In this recipe, we will see how the n parameter affects the number of generated responses and understand the different use cases for it.

How to do it...

1. In Postman, enter the following URL as the endpoint for chat completions: `https://api.openai.com/v1/chat/completions`.

2. In the request body, type in the following and click **Send**. Note that we have added the n parameter and set it to the default value of 1 explicitly:

    ```
    {
        "model": "gpt-3.5-turbo",
        "messages": [
            {
                "role": "user",
                "content": "Create a slogan for a company that sells
    Italian sandwiches"
            }
        ],
        "n": 1
    }
    ```

3. After sending the HTTP request, you should see the following (similar, but not exact) response from the OpenAI API:

    ```
    {
        "id": "chatcmpl-7rqKJ2fxKkltvcIpAPiNH1MUPMBIO",
        "object": "chat.completion",
        "created": 1693066883,
        "model": "gpt-3.5-turbo-0613",
        "choices": [
            {
                "index": 0,
                "message": {
    ```

```
                    "role": "assistant",
                    "content": "\"Indulge in the taste of Italy, one
    sandwich at a time.\""
                },
                "finish_reason": "stop"
            }
        ],
        "usage": {
            "prompt_tokens": 17,
            "completion_tokens": 16,
            "total_tokens": 33
        }
    }
```

4. Now, we'll repeat the request in *step 2*, but let's change the n parameter to a value of 3. After sending the HTTP request, we get the following response. Note that there are now three separate objects or responses within choices. We effectively received three different generated responses to the prompt:

```
    {
        "id": "chatcmpl-7rqc4P2PY6BxEhVF7gSGRXPkAtoKt",
        "object": "chat.completion",
        "created": 1693067984,
        "model": "gpt-3.5-turbo-0613",
        "choices": [
            {
                "index": 0,
                "message": {
                    "role": "assistant",
                    "content": "\"Indulge in authentic flavor with
    our heavenly Italian sandwiches!\""
                },
                "finish_reason": "stop"
            },
            {
                "index": 1,
                "message": {
                    "role": "assistant",
                    "content": "\"Deliciously Authentic: Taste Italy
    in Every Bite!\""
                },
                "finish_reason": "stop"
            },
            {
```

```
            "index": 2,
            "message": {
                "role": "assistant",
                "content": "\"Delizioso Flavors in Every
Bite!\""
            },
            "finish_reason": "stop"
        }
    ],
    "usage": {
        "prompt_tokens": 17,
        "completion_tokens": 35,
        "total_tokens": 52
    }
}
```

5. Now, let's generate images and observe how the n parameter affects the number of images returned. In Postman, enter the following for the endpoint: `https://api.openai.com/v1/images/generations`. In the request body, type in the following, and then click **Send**:

```
{
    "prompt": "Ice cream",
    "n": 3,
    "size": "1024x1024"
}
```

6. After sending the HTTP request, you should see the following response from the OpenAI API. Notably, you should see three different URLs, each corresponding to a generated image. The URLs in the following code block have been artificially condensed. After copying and pasting the URLs into your browser, you should see images of ice cream:

```
{
    "created": 1693068271,
    "data": [
        {
            "url": "https://oaidalleapiprodscus.blob.core.
windows.net/private/org-...%3D"
        },
        {
            "url": "https://oaidalleapiprodscus.blob.core.
windows.net/private/org-...s%3D"
        },
        {
            "url": "https://oaidalleapiprodscus.blob.core.
windows.net/private/org-...%3D"
```

```
            }
        ]
    }
```

Figure 3.1 – Output of the OpenAI image endpoint (n=3)

How it works...

The n parameter simply specifies the number of generated responses from the OpenAI API. For chat completions, it can be any integer; this means you can ask the API to return thousands and thousands of responses. For image generations, this parameter has a max value of *10*, meaning you can only generate up to 10 images per request.

Applications of n

The applications of having an n parameter are very broad – it's often useful to have a parameter that controls and repeats generations for the same prompt, all in one HTTP request. These include the following:

- **Creativity**: For creative apps and tasks such as slogan generation, songwriting, or brainstorming, providing a richer set of materials to work from makes it easier for users

- **Redundancy**: Since response generations from the OpenAI API with the same prompt can differ wildly, it's useful to create multiple responses and cross-verify the information, especially in mission-critical workflows

- **A/B testing**: Very common in marketing, the n parameter enables you to create multiple responses that users can experiment with to see which one performs better

Considerations of n

However, multiple generations do generally mean a lower speed and higher cost, which are considerations that need to be taken into account before deciding what value to set for the n parameter. For example, in our recipe, when we requested one generation, the cost was *33* tokens (as specified in the response). However, when n = 3, the total number of tokens jumped to *52* tokens. We learned in the previous recipe that the OpenAI API charges based on the total number of tokens generated.

Note that the cost increase is not linear – generating three additional responses only cost ~60% more tokens, instead of the expected 3x. This is for two reasons:

- The number of prompt tokens remains fixed no matter how many generations are created, whether it's 1 or 100
- The model finds computational savings when it knows to produce multiple completions instead of one

This is also why using the n parameter is far better (from a cost point of view) than just executing the HTTP request multiple times. Under the hood, when you set n = 3, the model in parallel processes the requests during a single model inference, leveraging inherent efficiencies. We could have, for example, run the HTTP request three times instead of one HTTP request where n = 3, but that would mean spending ~3x more cost and overhead.

Overall, the n parameter impacts the number of generated responses, which is tremendously valuable for particular use cases, resulting in lower costs as well.

Determining the randomness and creativity of generated responses using the temperature parameter

Temperature is likely to be one of the least understood parameters. Overall, it controls the creativity or randomness of text generations. The higher the temperature, the more diverse and creative the results will be – even for the same input. In practice, the temperature is set based on the use case. Applications where consistent and standard generations are needed should use a very low temperature, whereas solutions that require creative approaches should opt for higher temperatures.

In this recipe, we will learn about the temperature parameter, observing how it can be used to influence the text generations produced by the OpenAI API.

How to do it...

1. In Postman, enter the following for the endpoint: `https://api.openai.com/v1/chat/completions`. In the request body, type in the following, and then click **Send**. Our prompt is `Explain gravity in one sentence`. Note that we have added the `temperature` parameter and set it to the value of 0 explicitly. We will repeat this *three* times and record the responses of the `content` parameter for each generation:

```
{
    "model": "gpt-3.5-turbo",
    "messages": [
      {
        "role": "user",
        "content": "Explain gravity in one sentence"
      }
    ],
    "temperature": 0
}
```

```
# Response 1
Gravity is the force that attracts objects with mass towards
each other.
# Response 2
Gravity is the force that attracts objects with mass towards
each other.
# Response 3
Gravity is the force that attracts objects with mass towards
each other.
```

2. Next, let's edit our request body and change the `temperature` parameter to the highest value possible, which is 2. Click **Send**, and then repeat this three times, recording the responses of the `content` parameter for each generation:

```
{
    "model": "gpt-3.5-turbo",
    "messages": [
      {
        "role": "user",
        "content": "Explain gravity in one sentence"
      }
    ],
    "temperature": 2
}
```

```
# Response 1
```

```
Gravity is the force that attract objects with mass towards each
other, creating weight.
# Response 2
Gravity is a natural force that attracts objects toward each
other based on their mass and distance between them.
# Response 3
Gravity is the universal force of attraction that pulls every
object toward the Earth.
```

3. Now, let's repeat *steps 1–2* but use a more creative prompt, such as `Create a creative tag line for an AI learning book`. Again, we will first perform a chat completion with the temperature parameter equal to 0 three times. Then, we will increase the temperature parameter to 2 and run the request three times again. The responses of the `content` parameter for each generation are listed in the following code blocks. Note that yours will likely differ:

```
# Request Body

{
   "model": "gpt-3.5-turbo",
   "messages": [
      {
         "role": "user",
         "content": "Create a creative tag line for an AI learning
book"
      }
   ],
   "temperature": 0
}


# Response 1
Unlock the Power of Artificial Intelligence: Ignite Your Mind,
Transform Your Future!
# Response 2
Unlock the Power of Artificial Intelligence: Ignite Your Mind,
Transform Your Future!
# Response 3
Unlocking Minds, Unleashing Code: Navigating the Frontiers of AI
Learning


# Request Body

{
   "model": "gpt-3.5-turbo",
   "messages": [
      {
```

```
        "role": "user",
        "content": "Create a creative tag line for an AI learning
    book"
      }
    ],
    "temperature": 2
}


# Response 1
Spark your mind - Accelerate with Artificial Excellence.
# Response 2
Unlock limitless intelligence: Medium approach, myth together.
# Response 3
Unleashing Minds: The AI Odyssey Awaits.
```

How it works...

As we saw in the recipe, the temperature parameter controls the randomness and creativity of the text generation. When the temperature was set very low, the API produced very consistent and deterministic results for the same prompt. In the first example, gravity was explained in the same exact way for each chat completion:

```
Gravity is the force that attracts objects with mass towards each
other.
```

When we increased the temperature, we saw very different, more creative, and unexpected responses, such as the following:

```
Gravity is the universal force of attraction that pulls every object
toward the Earth.
```

Think of the temperature setting as the dial on a radio. A lower temperature is like tuning the radio to a well-established station where the signal is strong and clear, and you get a consistent, expected type of music or talk show. This is analogous to the model delivering responses that are reliable, straightforward, and closely aligned with the most likely answer.

Conversely, a higher temperature is similar to tuning the radio to a frequency where you might catch a variety of stations, some clear and some static-filled, playing an eclectic mix of genres. This creates an environment where unexpected, novel, and varied content comes through. In the context of the language model, this means generating more creative, diverse, and sometimes unpredictable responses, mirroring the eclectic and varied nature of a radio dial turned toward a less defined frequency.

Temperature inner working

As we discussed before, when a model generates text, it calculates probabilities for the next word based on the prompt and response it has built so far. In practice, temperature affects the response by changing the probability distribution of the next word.

With a higher temperature, this distribution becomes flatter, meaning less-probable words have a higher chance of being selected. At a lower temperature, the distribution becomes more pronounced or *sharper*, meaning the most probable words are likely to be chosen every time, which reduces randomness.

Decision based on use case

The decision on which temperature to use depends solely on the particular use case. In general, there are three categories of this parameter.

- **Low-temperature values (0.0 to 0.8)**: These should be used for primarily analytical, factual, or logical tasks so that the model is more deterministic and focused. In these use cases, traceability and repeatability is also important, and so a lower temperature is better, as it reduces randomness. A lower temperature also means adhering to established patterns and conventions, leading to more correct answers.

  Examples include generating code, performing data analysis, and answering factual questions.

- **Medium-temperature values (0.8 to 1.2)**: These should be used for general-purpose and chatbot-like tasks, where balancing coherence and creativity is critical. This enables the model to be flexible and produce new ideas, but it still remains focused to the prompt at-hand.

  Examples include chatbots/conversational agents and Q&A systems.

- **High-temperature values (1.2 to 2.0)**: These should be used for creative writing and brainstorming as the model is not constrained to follow established patterns and can explore very diverse styles. Here, a *correct* answer does not exist, and instead, the purpose is to create varying outputs. This does mean that you may get unexpected outputs that do not conform to the actual prompt at all.

  Examples include storytelling, generating marketing slogans, and brainstorming company names.

In the recipe, a lower temperature was far better when explaining gravity, as the prompt encourages a factual and straightforward answer. However, the second prompt, about creating a tagline, is far better suited for a higher temperature, as this is a task that requires creativity and out-of-the-box thinking.

Overall, setting a temperature value means performing a trade-off between coherence and creativity, which shifts based on how you use the API within your application. As a rule of thumb, it's best to set the temperature to 1 and then modify it in increments of 0.2 until you reach your desired output set.

4

Incorporating Additional Features from the OpenAI API

The OpenAI API offers additional features beyond the standard endpoints and parameters that we learned about in the previous chapter. These provide additional customizability to the existing model and enable far more use cases by linking the model to other methods.

In particular, the OpenAI API contains a robust embedding model, enabling users to vectorize text to perform typical NLP functions such as text clustering, text classification, text comparison, and more. This is the same technology that search engines such as Google use, for example, to return relevant search results. Now, with the OpenAI API, it is available at your fingertips.

The API also contains a method to *fine-tune* or customize a model for a particular use case. Instead of the fine-tuning we did earlier, which required *priming* the model with several examples, this is a better and typically cheaper alternative.

Finally, the API also possesses the ability to create **function calls**. This enables you to provide the API with a set of functions and their descriptions, and the model in turn intelligently creates a JSON object containing arguments to call that function, enabling you to link the OpenAI API to any user-defined functions.

However, in order to use these features, we need to call the API through a programmatic language such as *Python* instead of through one-time HTTP requests such as Postman. As a result, we will first cover how to use the OpenAI API with Python instead of Postman, and then learn about the benefits that this change in methodology enables.

By the end of this chapter, you will know how to use these features in your applications. This is important because understanding these features will open up a plethora of other use cases that would otherwise not be possible to execute. Additionally, we will cover applications of each feature beyond what is covered within each recipe.

In this chapter, we will cover the following recipes:

- Using the Python library to call the OpenAI API

- Using the embedding model for text comparison and other use cases

- Fine-tuning a completion model and relevant applications

Technical requirements

All the recipes in this chapter require you to have access to the OpenAI API (via a generated API key) and have an API client installed. In case you don't recall how to do this, you can refer to the *Chapter 1* recipe *Making OpenAI API requests with Postman*.

In previous chapters, we have used Postman as our API client. In this case, we will use the programmatic language Python instead. Specifically, the recipes will use the OpenAI Python library to make calls to the OpenAI API.

We will run Python in a service called **Google Colab**. Colab is an online hosted **Jupyter Notebook** service by Google, that requires no setup to use and can run Python code within the browser. The Jupyter Notebook is an open sourced web application that allows you to create and share documents and contains live code that can be run step by step. This is the environment we will use to run our Python code.

To use Google Colab, you need to create and be signed in to a valid Google account, which is completely free. Follow the steps to create a new Google account at `https://accounts.google.com/`.

Using the Python library to call the OpenAI API

Previously, we used HTTP requests and Postman to call the OpenAI API. Now, we are transferring to another method of calling the API, through Python with the dedicated OpenAI Python library. Why does this matter and why is this important?

Utilizing the Python library for OpenAI API calls offers a significant advantage over manual HTTP requests in tools such as Postman, especially for developers looking to integrate ChatGPT functionality into their applications seamlessly.

Python's library simplifies the intricacies involved in making direct HTTP requests by offering a more user-friendly and intuitive interface. This facilitates quick prototyping, streamlined error management, and efficient parsing of responses. The library wraps the fundamental details of the protocol, allowing developers to concentrate on their application's essential functionality without being bogged down by the specifics of request headers, query strings, and HTTP methods.

Furthermore, Python's extensive package ecosystem readily supports the integration of the OpenAI API with other services and systems, allowing for a scalable and maintainable code base.

Overall, if you are serious about building intelligent applications with the OpenAI API, you need to call the API with a programmatic language that enables complex logic and tie-ins to other systems. Python, through the OpenAI library, is one way to accomplish that.

In this recipe, we will create some simple API calls using Python and the OpenAI library. More information on the library can be found here: https://github.com/openai/openai-python.

Getting ready

Ensure you have an OpenAI platform account with available usage credits. If you don't, please follow the *Setting up your OpenAI Playground environment* recipe in *Chapter 1*.

Furthermore, ensure you are logged in to a Google account and have access to a notebook. You can verify this by going to https://colab.google/ and selecting **New Notebook** at the top right. After that, you should have a blank screen with an empty notebook open.

All the recipes in this chapter have the same requirements.

How to do it...

1. In your Google Colab notebook, click the first empty cell, and type in the following code to download and install the OpenAI Python library. After you have typed the code in, press *Shift + Enter* to run the code inside the cell. Alternatively, you can run the code inside the cell by clicking the **Play** button to the left of the cell. This code will attempt to install the OpenAI Python library and all its dependencies. You may see output such as Requirements already satisfied or Installing httpcore. This is Google attempting to install the libraries that OpenAI depends on to run its own library, and is perfectly normal:

```
!pip install openai
from openai import OpenAI
```

2. Ensure that the words Successfully installed openai-X.XX.X are visible, as seen in *Figure 4.1*.

```
!pip install openai
from openai import OpenAI

Collecting openai
  Downloading openai-1.10.0-py3-none-any.whl (225 kB)
  ────────────────────────────────────── 225.1/225.1 kB 2.3 MB/s eta 0:00:00
Requirement already satisfied: anyio<5,>=3.5.0 in /usr/local/lib/python3.10/dist-packages (from openai) (3.7.1)
Requirement already satisfied: distro<2,>=1.7.0 in /usr/lib/python3/dist-packages (from openai) (1.7.0)
Collecting httpx<1,>=0.23.0 (from openai)
  Downloading httpx-0.26.0-py3-none-any.whl (75 kB)
  ────────────────────────────────────── 75.9/75.9 kB 3.7 MB/s eta 0:00:00
Requirement already satisfied: pydantic<3,>=1.9.0 in /usr/local/lib/python3.10/dist-packages (from openai) (1.10.14)
Requirement already satisfied: sniffio in /usr/local/lib/python3.10/dist-packages (from openai) (1.3.0)
Requirement already satisfied: tqdm>4 in /usr/local/lib/python3.10/dist-packages (from openai) (4.66.1)
Collecting typing-extensions<5,>=4.7 (from openai)
  Downloading typing_extensions-4.9.0-py3-none-any.whl (32 kB)
Requirement already satisfied: idna>=2.8 in /usr/local/lib/python3.10/dist-packages (from anyio<5,>=3.5.0->openai) (3.6)
Requirement already satisfied: exceptiongroup in /usr/local/lib/python3.10/dist-packages (from anyio<5,>=3.5.0->openai) (1.2.0)
Requirement already satisfied: certifi in /usr/local/lib/python3.10/dist-packages (from httpx<1,>=0.23.0->openai) (2023.11.17)
Collecting httpcore==1.* (from httpx<1,>=0.23.0->openai)
  Downloading httpcore-1.0.2-py3-none-any.whl (76 kB)
  ────────────────────────────────────── 76.9/76.9 kB 3.0 MB/s eta 0:00:00
Collecting h11<0.15,>=0.13 (from httpcore==1.*->httpx<1,>=0.23.0->openai)
  Downloading h11-0.14.0-py3-none-any.whl (58 kB)
  ────────────────────────────────────── 58.3/58.3 kB 2.4 MB/s eta 0:00:00
Installing collected packages: typing-extensions, h11, httpcore, httpx, openai
  Attempting uninstall: typing-extensions
    Found existing installation: typing_extensions 4.5.0
    Uninstalling typing_extensions-4.5.0:
      Successfully uninstalled typing_extensions-4.5.0
ERROR: pip's dependency resolver does not currently take into account all the packages that are installed. This behaviour is the source of the following dependency conflicts.
llmx 0.0.15a0 requires cohere, which is not installed.
llmx 0.0.15a0 requires tiktoken, which is not installed.
tensorflow-probability 0.22.0 requires typing-extensions<4.6.0, but you have typing-extensions 4.9.0 which is incompatible.
Successfully installed h11-0.14.0 httpcore-1.0.2 httpx-0.26.0 openai-1.10.0 typing-extensions-4.9.0
```

Figure 4.1 – Output of Jupyter notebook after installing the OpenAI library

3. Next, we need to perform authentication. This is similar to the previous chapters where we had to authenticate our Postman requests by putting our API key in a **Header** parameter called *Authorization*. In Python, it's much simpler. In the cell below the one you used in *step 1*, write the following code and press *Shift + Enter*. Note, replace `<api-key>` with the API key that you generated in the last recipe in *Chapter 1*:

```
api_key = "<api-key>"
client = OpenAI(api_key=api_key)
```

4. We will now make a chat completion request to the OpenAI API. Similar to Postman, we can use different endpoints and define a variety of different parameters within the request in Python. Type the following code into a new cell below and press *Shift + Enter*, which runs the code and saves the output in a variable called `completion`:

```
completion = client.chat.completions.create(
    model="gpt-3.5-turbo",
    messages=[
        {'role': 'system', 'content': 'You are an assistant that
creates a slogan based on company description'},
        {"role": "user", "content": "A company that sells ice
cream"}
    ],
    n=1,
    temperature=1
)
```

5. Output the `completion` variable, which is a `ChatCompletion` object. We can convert this into the more familiar JSON format (exactly as in Postman) by typing the following in the cell below and running the code by pressing *Shift + Enter*:

```
import json
completion_json = json.loads(completion.json())
print(completion_json)
```

Figure 4.2 shows the output that you will see after running this code.

```
{'id': 'chatcmpl-8PH66gfwlJK8cEaxp9YICRlc63wa4',
 'choices': [{'finish_reason': 'stop',
   'index': 0,
   'message': {'content': '"Indulge in Delightful Bliss with Our Creamy Delights!"',
    'role': 'assistant',
    'function_call': None,
    'tool_calls': None}}],
 'created': 1701034614,
 'model': 'gpt-3.5-turbo-0613',
 'object': 'chat.completion',
 'system_fingerprint': None,
 'usage': {'completion_tokens': 16, 'prompt_tokens': 29, 'total_tokens': 45}}
```

Figure 4.2 – JSON output of the Python OpenAI completion request

6. Using Python, we can parse through the JSON and only output the part of the JSON that contains the company slogan. We can do this by typing the following code into the cell below and pressing *Shift + Enter* to run the code:

```
print(completion_json['choices'][0]['message']['content'])
```

```
print(completion_json['choices'][0]['message']['content'])

"Indulge in Delightful Bliss with Our Creamy Delights!"
```

Figure 4.3 – Input and output of step 6

7. You now have a working Python Jupyter notebook that calls the OpenAI API, makes a chat completion request, and outputs the result.

How it works…

In this recipe, we performed the same actions as we have done in previous recipes, the difference being that we used the OpenAI Python library instead of invoking HTTP requests through Postman. We authenticated using our API key, made a chat completion request, and adjusted several parameters (such as *Model*, *Messages*, *N*, and *Temperature*), and printed the output result.

Code walk-through

The code that was run within the recipe can be explained in four parts:

- *Library installation*: The first line – `!pip install openai; import openai` – is a command that installs the OpenAI library as a package in Python. The second line imports it into the current Python namespace, enabling the use of the library's functions and classes.

- *Authentication*: The `openai.api_key = "sk-..."` line sets the API key for authenticating requests to the OpenAI API.

- *API call*: The `openai.ChatCompletion.create()` line calls the API and makes a chat completion request. As you can see, it contains the typical parameters that we have discussed in previous chapters.

- *Output*: The `print(completion); print(completion['choices'][0]['message']['content'])` line prints out the raw response from the API call. The response includes not only the content of the completion but also some metadata, similar to when we make HTTP requests with Postman. This second line digs into the response object to extract and print only the content of the message.

Most API calls in Python follow these steps. It should be noted that *steps 1 and 2* (i.e., library installation and authentication) only need to be performed once. This is because once a library is installed, it becomes a part of your Python environment, ready to be used in any program without needing to be reinstalled each time. Similarly, authentication, which is often a process of verifying credentials to gain access to the API, is typically required only once per session or configuration, as your credentials are then stored and reused for subsequent API calls.

Overall, we delved into using the OpenAI Python library for interacting with the OpenAI API, transitioning from the HTTP requests method in Postman. We will continue following this process in future recipes.

Components of the Python library

The endpoints and parameters that we have discussed in previous chapters are all available within the OpenAI Python library. The syntax is slightly different, as we are now using Python code rather than JSON (through Postman) to make API requests, but the fundamental idea is the same. Here is a table that compares endpoint calls between Postman and Python libraries.

Endpoint	HTTP request in Postman through JSON (the Body component)	Python OpenAI Library

Chat completions	<pre>{
	    "model": "gpt-3.5-tur-
	bo",
	    "messages": [
	        {
	            "role": "system",
	            "content": "You
	are a helpful assistant."
	        },
	        {
	            "role": "user",
	            "content": "Hel-
	lo!"
	        }
	    ]
	}</pre>
		<pre>completion = cli-
		ent.chat.comple-
		tions.create (
		    mod-
		el="gpt-3.5-tur-
		bo",
		    messages=[
		        {"role": "sys-
		tem", "content":
		"You are a helpful
		assistant."},
		        {"role":
		"user", "content":
		"Hello!"}
		    ]
		)</pre>

Images	<pre>{
	    "prompt": "A cute baby
	sea otter",
	    "n": 2,
	    "size": "1024x1024"
	}</pre>
		<pre>client.images.gen-
		erate(
		    prompt="A cute
		baby sea otter",
		    n=2,
		    size="1024x1024"
		)</pre>

Audio	<pre>-F file="@/path/to/file/
	audio.mp3" \
	    -F model="whisper-1"</pre>
		<pre>audio_file =
		open("audio.mp3",
		"rb")
		transcript = cli-
		ent.audio.tran-
		scriptions.cre-
		ate ("whisper-1",
		audio_file)</pre>

Table 4.1 – Comparing endpoint calls between Postman and Python libraries

Benefits and drawbacks of using the Python library

There are several benefits to doing this, aside from it just being a pre-requisite to future recipes. It provides abstraction over the API request itself, leading to the following benefits:

- *Simplified authentication*: The library handles API key and token management, abstracting away the details of the authentication process from the user. For example, in this case, we did not need to create a new parameter for *Bearer*, unlike within HTTP. Furthermore, unlike HTTP requests, we do not need to declare our API key for every single request.

- *Ease of use*: It provides a high-level interface with methods and classes that represent API endpoints, making it easier to understand and implement; the library takes care of constructing the correct HTTP requests, encoding parameters, and parsing the responses.

- *Do more*: The library often includes convenience features that are not available with simple HTTP requests, such as pagination helpers, streaming, session management, embeddings, function calls, and more (which is why we switched over to the Python library in this chapter – the subsequent recipes cover these features).

- *Programmability*: The Python OpenAI library leverages the full programming capabilities of Python, enabling variables, logical conditioning, and functions (i.e., all the benefits of a programming language that you don't get with Postman).

There are, however, some specific downsides to using the Python library as well:

- *Limited customization*: High-level abstraction may limit direct access to certain API functionalities

- *Maintenance and compatibility*: There is a dependency on library updates and potential conflicts with different Python versions

- *Performance overheads*: Additional abstraction layers can lead to slower performance in resource-critical applications

- *Reduced control*: It offers less flexibility for users needing detailed control over API interactions

Using the embedding model for text comparisons and other use cases

OpenAI has a model and endpoint that enables users to create **embeddings**. It's a lesser-known feature of the API but has vast applications in enabling plenty of use cases (searching through text, text classification, and much more).

What are embeddings? **Text embedding** is a sophisticated technique employed in NLP that transforms text into a numerical format that machines can understand. Essentially, embeddings are high-dimensional vectors that capture the essence of words, sentences, or even entire documents, encapsulating not just their individual meanings but also the nuances and relationships between them.

Mathematically, a vector is a point in an n-dimensional vector space, but for our purposes, you can think of a vector as just a list of numbers. However, the recipes discussed in this chapter do not require you to work with the process and science behind converting words to numbers. For more information on the science behind embeddings, you can find a great introductory article here: `https://stackoverflow.blog/2023/11/09/an-intuitive-introduction-to-text-embeddings/`.

In this recipe, we will use the OpenAI API to convert various texts into embeddings and use those embeddings for the use case of text comparison.

How to do it...

1. Open up a new notebook by navigating to `https://colab.google/` and selecting **New Notebook** at the top right.

2. In the first cell, type in the following code and press *Shift + Enter* to run the code. This will install the OpenAI library and import the required modules for this recipe:

```
!pip install openai
from openai import OpenAI
from numpy import dot
from numpy.linalg import norm
```

3. Similar to the previous recipe, type the following code into the cell below, replacing `<api-key>` with your OpenAI API Key. Hit *Shift + Enter* to run the code:

```
api_key = "<Insert your API-key here>"
client = OpenAI(api_key=api_key)
```

4. Next, we will create two functions in Python. The first function will create an embedding given a text string. To do this, we will use the **Embeddings** endpoint from the OpenAI API. The next function takes two embeddings and calculates the difference between them using **cosine similarity**, a concept that we will discuss in the next section. To do this, type the following code in the cell below and press *Shift + Enter*:

```
def create_embeddings(text):
    embedding = client.embeddings.create(input=text, model="text-
embedding-ada-002").data[0].embedding
    return embedding

def compare_two_embeddings(a, b):
    cos_sim = dot(a, b)/(norm(a)*norm(b))
    return cos_sim
```

5. Now, we have everything we need to start comparing texts by creating embeddings and calculating the difference between them. Let's start with two pieces of text that are semantically very similar: *I like apples* and *I like bananas*. Type in the following code, hit *Shift + Enter*, and note the output result:

```
text_1 = "I like apples"
text_2 = "I like bananas"
round(compare_two_embeddings(create_embeddings(text_1), create_
embeddings(text_2)), 2)
```

```
[14] text_1 = "I like apples"
     text_2 = "I like bananas"
     round(compare_two_embeddings(create_embeddings(text_1), create_embeddings(text_2)), 2)

     0.9
```

Figure 4.4 – Output of cosine similarity for similar texts

6. Next, let's compare two pieces of text that are not similar: *I like apples* and the first section of Article 1 of the US Constitution: *All legislative Powers herein granted shall be vested in a Congress of the United States, which shall consist of a Senate and House of Representatives* (https://www.archives.gov/founding-docs/constitution-transcript). Type in the following code, hit *Shift + Enter*, and note the output result:

```
text_1 = "I like apples"
text_2 = "All legislative Powers herein granted shall be vested
in a Congress of the United States, which shall consist of a
Senate and House of Representatives."
round(compare_two_embeddings(create_embeddings(text_1), create_
embeddings(text_2)), 2)
```

```
[15] text_1 = "I like apples"
     text_2 = "All legislative Powers herein granted shall be vested in a Congress of the \
             United States, which shall consist of a Senate and House of Representatives."
     round(compare_two_embeddings(create_embeddings(text_1), create_embeddings(text_2)), 2)

     0.7
```

Figure 4.5 – Output of cosine similarity for similar texts

7. Note the similarity between the first set of texts (0.90) was higher than for the next set of texts (0.70). This means that the first set of texts is more semantically similar than the next two texts, which makes sense given the language.

8.   Let's take this one step further. Repeat *steps 5-7* with the following texts. I've also noted the output similarities I got:

```
text_1 = "Birds like to fly"
text_2 = "Airplanes can soar above the ground"
Output = 0.88

text_1 = "Birds like to fly"
text_2 = "A fly can irritate me"
Output = 0.84
```

How it works...

In this recipe, we converted texts into embeddings and then compared the embeddings. The results showed us that, when comparing it to *I like applies*, the text *I like bananas* is more semantically similar to the first section of the US Constitution.

Furthermore, it demonstrated that the text *Birds like to fly* is more semantically similar to *Airplanes can soar above the ground* than *A fly can irritate me*. This makes sense as in the first two pieces of text, the sentences were about objects flying.

Embedding 101

As mentioned before, the process of embedding turns text into a list of numbers. This is imperative in NLP, as now machines can work with these lists of numbers instead of text.

The key feature of OpenAI's embedding model is that it captures linguistic properties and semantic meaning. This means that two pieces of text that are semantically similar will have similar vectors (i.e., a similar list of numbers). **Semantically similar** means that two pieces of text convey the same or related meanings, concepts, or ideas, even if they use different words or structures.

Code structure

We used OpenAI's embedding model to create these vectors, using the Embeddings endpoint. The endpoint can be called with the `openai.Embedding.create()` function, and takes in two arguments:

- `input`: This argument represents the text that you want to create embeddings for.
- `model`: This is the ID of the model you want to use for the embeddings. This is similar to the `model` parameter in other endpoints. In this example, we used the standard **ada** model, which was `text-embedding-ada-002`. OpenAI recommends using this as the starting embedding model as it's quite affordable and still has excellent performance.

The function call returns an embedding object in JSON format, which we then parse through to get the embedding itself (which again is a list of numbers in Python). The parsing is done via the `["data"]` `[0]["embedding"]` code.

After we have the embeddings from two sets of text, we then need to compare them. How do you compare two vectors (i.e., how do you compare two lists of numbers?)? The most common method used is called **cosine similarity**. Cosine similarity measures the cosine of the angle between two vectors, resulting in a number between 0 and 1.

Cosine similarity is often chosen over other similarity measuring techniques because it is particularly effective in high-dimensional spaces, such as text data, where it emphasizes the orientation rather than the magnitude of vectors. This approach allows it to focus on the directional alignment of the vectors, making it more robust in assessing the semantic similarity between texts, even when they vary in length or word frequency.

The math does not matter here – the implication is that the higher the cosine similarity, the more closely the two texts are semantically related:

- *Cosine similarity close to 1*: The texts are very similar or have similar context or meaning
- *Cosine similarity close to 0*: The texts are unrelated
- *Cosine similarity close to -1*: The texts are semantically opposite, which is rare in NLP because most text embeddings are designed to have non-negative components

In Python, this is achieved through the following code, which takes the dot product of the two vectors and divides it by the product of the two vectors' Euclidean norm:

```
def compare_two_embeddings(a, b):
    cos_sim = dot(a, b)/(norm(a)*norm(b))
    return cos_sim
```

After we set up a function to return the embeddings for each text, and the function to compute the cosine similarity between two embeddings, we had all the tools we needed to compare two pieces of text.

The normalization in this formula (`norm`) ensures that we're comparing the direction, rather than the magnitude, of the two vectors. This means we are focusing on how similar the two vectors are in terms of orientation, regardless of their length, which is essential for measuring similarity in many applications such as comparing sentences.

Applications in text comparison

Embeddings are an efficient way to compare two pieces of text, opening lots of different real-world applications. Recall the similarity scores that were computed in the recipe, described in the table that follows:

Test	Base text	Comparison text	Cosine similarity of embeddings
1	I like apples	I like bananas	0.90
		All legislative Powers herein granted shall be vested in a Congress of the United States, which shall consist of a Senate and House of Representatives	0.71
2	Birds like to fly	Airplanes can soar above the ground	0.88
		A fly can irritate me	0.84

Table 4.2 – Cosine similarities between OpenAI embeddings for various sets of texts

The OpenAI API enables you to compute and rank the semantic similarity between different sets of text. Note that semantic similarity understands the nuances of the meaning of the text. In *Test 2*, the semantic similarity to *Airplanes can soar above the ground* was greater than *A fly can irritate me*.

This is counterintuitive because you would assume that the text that shares the word *fly* would be more similar. However, the embeddings recognize that the word *fly* is used in a different context in *Birds like to fly* versus *A fly can irritate me*. In this case, embeddings are powerful mechanisms to compare the meanings of texts.

There are other applications of embeddings that, thanks to OpenAI API, you can explore when building apps. This is not an exhaustive list but should be a good start for you to get some idea about the API's potential:

- *Information retrieval with search engines*: Enhancing search algorithms to return results that are semantically related to the query, not just textually (`https://www.mage.ai/blog/building-semantic-search-engine-with-dual-space-word-embeddings`)

- *Document retrieval*: Finding documents that cover similar topics even if they don't share the same keywords (`https://arxiv.org/pdf/1810.10176v2.pdf`)

- *Content recommendation systems*: Recommending articles, products, or media to users based on semantic similarity to items they have liked before (`https://towardsdatascience.com/introduction-to-embedding-based-recommender-systems-956faceb1919`)

- *Text classification*: Automatically classifying documents into predefined categories based on their semantic content (`https://realpython.com/python-keras-text-classification/`)

Overall, the embeddings feature of the OpenAI API opens a plethora of other use cases, from text comparison to information retrieval. Another key benefit is that these endpoints are far cheaper than the Completions or Images endpoint, making it a powerful and efficient tool in your arsenal.

Fine-tuning a completion model

Fine-tuning is the process of taking a pre-trained model and further adapting it to a specific task or dataset. The goal is typically to take an original model that has been trained on a large, general dataset and apply it to a more specialized domain or to improve its performance on a specific type of data.

We previously saw a version of fine-tuning in the first recipe within *Chapter 1*, where we added examples of outputs in the `messages` parameter to *fine-tune* the output response. In this case, the model had not technically been fine-tuned – we instead performed **few-shot learning**, where we gave examples of the output within the prompt itself to the Chat Completion model. Fine-tuning, however, is a process where a whole new subset Chat Completion model is created with training data (inputs and outputs).

In this recipe, we will explore how to fine-tune a model and execute that fine-tuned model. Then, we will discuss the benefits and drawbacks of fine-tuning a model with the OpenAI API.

How to do it...

1. Open up a new notebook by navigating to `https://colab.google/` and selecting **New Notebook** at the top right.

2. In the first cell, type in the following code and press *Shift + Enter* to run the code. This will install the OpenAI library and import the required modules for this recipe:

    ```
    !pip install openai
    from openai import OpenAI
    import os
    ```

3. Similar to the previous recipe, type the following code into the cell below, replacing `<api-key>` with your OpenAI API key. Hit *Shift + Enter* to run the code:

    ```
    api_key = "<Insert your API-key here>"
    client = OpenAI(api_key=api_key)
    ```

4. Import the training data into Google Colab. The training data file can be found here: `https://drive.google.com/file/d/1x0ciWtW3phjPHAosiCL90qsQY--ZoxsV/view?usp=sharing`. To upload the file into Google Colab, select the *Files* icon on the left and select the **Upload File** button at the top of that menu. Both these icons have been highlighted in *Figure 4.6*. Note that the training data includes several examples of where the prompt is a scenario (such as *A student in a library*) and the completion is a one-liner joke followed by *Haha* (such as *Why did the student bring a ladder to the library? Because they heard the knowledge was on the top shelf! Haha*).

Figure 4.6 – How to add a file to Google Colab

5. Next, upload the training dataset to the OpenAI API, by typing in the following code and hitting *Shift + Enter*. We will also retrieve `file_id` from the upload:

```
training_data = client.files.create(
  file=open("chapter4trainingdata.json", "rb"),
  purpose='fine-tune'
)
file_id = training_data.id
```

6. After that, we will begin fine-tuning the model, by typing in the following code and hitting *Shift + Enter*. This will begin the fine-tuning process, by instructing OpenAI to use the file that we had previously uploaded through the `file_id` variable:

```
fine_tune_job = client.fine_tuning.jobs.create(training_
file=file_id, model="gpt-3.5-turbo")
```

7. Fine-tuning can take several minutes to finish. We can check the status of the job by typing in the following code and hitting *Shift + Enter*. If the output is *running*, that means the fine-tuning is still in process. Wait until the following code returns `succeeded`:

```
client.fine_tuning.jobs.retrieve(fine_tune_job.id).status
```

8. Now that the fine-tuning job has been completed, we need the name of the fine-tuned model, which we can get by typing in the following code and hitting *Shift + Enter*. We will save this to the `fine_tuned_model` variable:

```
fine_tuned_model = client.fine_tuning.jobs.retrieve(fine_tune_
job.id).fine_tuned_model
```

9. Next, let's use our fine-tuned model. Let's create a simple chat completion request, but we will modify the `model` parameter to use the `fine_tuned_model` object that we had just created:

```
Completion = client.chat.completions.create(
  model=fine_tuned_model,
  messages=[
    {"role": "system", "content": "You are an assistant that
creates funny one-line jokes based on a given scenario."},
      {"role": "user", "content": "A man walking across the
road"}
    ]
)
print(completion.choices[0].message)
```

```
[16] completion = client.chat.completions.create(
    model=fine_tuned_model,
    messages=[
      {"role": "system", "content": "You are an assistant that creates funny one-line jokes based on a given scenario."},
      {"role": "user", "content": "A man walking across the road"}
    ]
  )
print(completion.choices[0].message.content)

Why did the man start skipping while walking across the road? Because his favorite song came on! Haha
```

Figure 4.7 – Chat completion request and output when using a fine-tuned model

10. Note that without providing any examples, the completion output is a one-liner joke followed by the word `Haha`. We successfully fine-tuned a model and then used the fine-tuned model.

How it works...

In this recipe, we created a fine-tuned model by providing the OpenAI API with training data that taught the model how it should respond to prompts. In this case, we trained it so that its output should be a one-liner joke followed by the word `Haha`. We then changed the `model` parameter to the ID of the model we just created, and made a *chat completion* request. After that, we noted that the output we received on a prompt it had never seen before also resulted in a one-liner joke followed by the word `Haha`. In essence, we had successfully fine-tuned the *gpt-3.5-turbo* model to tell one-liner jokes given any prompt.

Fine-tuning steps

There are five steps that need to be followed when fine-tuning a model and then using that fine-tuned model:

- *Prepare a training data file*: The training data consists of examples or prompts and desired completions. You need at least 10 examples to successfully train a model. Each example looks very similar (with purposeful intent) to the `messages` parameter when making a chat completion request. The difference, however, is that it also includes the completion (also known as the output from the assistant). Here is an example:

```
{"messages": [{"role": "system", "content": "You are an
assistant that creates funny one-line jokes based on a given
scenario."}, {"role": "user", "content": "A student in a
library"}, {"role": "assistant", "content": "Why did the student
bring a ladder to the library? Because they heard the knowledge
was on the top shelf! Haha"}]}
```

These examples can be added to a JSON file, with each line representing one example.

```
1  {"messages": [{"role": "system", "content": "You are an assistant that creates funny one-line jokes based on a given
   scenario."}, {"role": "user", "content": "A student in a library"}, {"role": "assistant", "content": "Why did the
   student bring a ladder to the library? Because they heard the knowledge was on the top shelf! Haha"}]}
2  {"messages": [{"role": "system", "content": "You are an assistant that creates funny one-line jokes based on a given
   scenario."}, {"role": "user", "content": "A cat sitting on a computer keyboard"}, {"role": "assistant", "content": "Why
   don't cats work on computers? Because they keep pressing 'paws'! Haha"}]}
3  {"messages":[{"role":"system","content":"You are an assistant that creates funny one-line jokes based on a given
   scenario."},{"role":"user","content":"A chef who over-salts everything"},{"role":"assistant","content":"Why did the
   chef start a rock band? Because he was all about that bass, no treble! Haha"}]}
4  {"messages":[{"role":"system","content":"You are an assistant that creates funny one-line jokes based on a given
   scenario."},{"role":"user","content":"A knight getting ready for a battle"},{"role":"assistant","content":"Why was the
   knight always calm before battle? Because he was good at keeping his 'armor' cool! Haha"}]}
5  {"messages":[{"role":"system","content":"You are an assistant that creates funny one-line jokes based on a given
   scenario."},{"role":"user","content":"A clown at a job interview"},{"role":"assistant","content":"Why did the clown
   bring a pie to the interview? He heard it was important to break the ice! Haha"}]}
6  {"messages":[{"role":"system","content":"You are an assistant that creates funny one-line jokes based on a given
   scenario."},{"role":"user","content":"A vampire at a blood drive"},{"role":"assistant","content":"Why did the vampire
   go to the blood drive? To improve his LinkedIn 'connections'! Haha"}]}
7  {"messages":[{"role":"system","content":"You are an assistant that creates funny one-line jokes based on a given
   scenario."},{"role":"user","content":"A pirate walking into a bar"},{"role":"assistant","content":"Why did the pirate
   walk into a bar? Because he heard they had a 'captain's special' on the 'high seas'! Haha"}]}
8  {"messages":[{"role":"system","content":"You are an assistant that creates funny one-line jokes based on a given
   scenario."},{"role":"user","content":"A dinosaur learning to dance"},{"role":"assistant","content":"Why did the
   dinosaur take up salsa? Because the 'Tyrannosaurus Flex' was already his signature move! Haha"}]}
9  {"messages":[{"role":"system","content":"You are an assistant that creates funny one-line jokes based on a given
   scenario."},{"role":"user","content":"An astronaut doing laundry"},{"role":"assistant","content":"Why did the astronaut
   bring soap into space? Because he wanted to rocket clean! Haha"}]}
10 {"messages":[{"role":"system","content":"You are an assistant that creates funny one-line jokes based on a given
   scenario."},{"role":"user","content":"A wizard at the supermarket"},{"role":"assistant","content":"Why did the wizard
   shop at the supermarket? Because the 'produce' section was truly enchanting! Haha"}]}
```

Figure 4.8 – Image of JSON file containing training data

- *Import to OpenAI*: After the training file has been made, it needs to be uploaded to OpenAI's servers, which is what we did with the following code:

```
training_data = client.files.create(
   file=open("chapter4trainingdata.json", "rb"),
   purpose='fine-tune'
)
```

- *Assign an ID*: After uploading the file, the API assigns it an ID. This ID can be determined by looking at the response JSON from the preceding code, and parsing for the `id` parameter:

```
file_id = training_data.id
```

- *Fine-tune the model*: After that, we need to instruct the API to fine-tune the model using the uploaded training data. We will put the response that we get from the API in a variable:

```
fine_tune_job = client.fine_tuning.jobs.create(training_
file=file_id, model="gpt-3.5-turbo")
```

Fine-tuning can take several minutes. We can check the status of our fine-tuning job through another API call and then parse through the response object:

```
client.fine_tuning.jobs.retrieve(fine_tune_job.id).status
```

After the fine-tuning job is complete, the API will assign a `fine_tuned_model` parameter, giving the fine-tuned model a particular identifier, which we can store in a variable:

```
fine_tuned_model = client.fine_tuning.jobs.retrieve(fine_tune_
job.id).fine_tuned_model
```

- *Use the fine-tuned model*: The last step is fairly easy – call the Chat Completions API as normal but modify the `model` parameter to the newly fine-tuned model that was just created:

```
completion = client.chat.completions.create(
  model=fine_tuned_model,
  messages=[
    {"role": "system", "content": "You are an assistant that
creates funny one-line jokes based on a given scenario."},
    {"role": "user", "content": "A man walking across the
road"}
  ]
)
print(completion.choices[0].message.content)
```

Benefits of fine-tuning

Fine-tuning improves few-shot learning by allowing you to train on many more examples than what would fit in a typical prompt context window. Once a model has been tuned, these examples are not needed every single time when making a completions request, thereby saving tokens (and costs) and resulting in lower latency (i.e., faster speed). Recall that tokens are the smallest units of meaning in a piece of text (typically words, punctuation marks, or other elements) used in NLP and often form the basis of how OpenAI charges chat completion requests.

For example, let's go through the number of tokens for two models (i) one that uses the *gpt-3.5* base model without any fine-tuning, but we need to include examples in the prompt every time, and (ii) a fine-tuned model.

Model	Gpt-3.5	Gpt-3.5 that has been fine-tuned
Prompt	You are an assistant who creates funny one-line jokes based on a given scenario. Here are 10 examples: A knight getting ready for a battle → Why was the knight always calm before battle? Because he was good at keeping his "armor" cool! Haha ... [9 more examples] ... Scenario: A penguin in the Arctic	You are an assistant who creates funny one-line jokes based on a given scenario. Scenario: A penguin in the Arctic
Number of tokens in prompt (estimated)	400	36

Table 4.3 – Comparison of prompt examples and number of tokens
between a non-fine-tuned and a fine-tuned GPT-3.5 model

A fine-tuned model uses about one-tenth of the number of tokens as the few-shot base model. This means that using a fine-tuned model can result in 90% cost savings, which can be very high if you deploy these models to heavily used applications.

Other benefits of fine-tuning include higher-quality results by being able to train on thousands of examples, which is not possible using few-shot learning as there is a maximum length for the prompt.

> **Note**
>
> Fine-tuning a model to get better-quality results should only be done after sufficient attempts at prompt engineering and prompt chaining have been made. Fine-tuning a model requires significant resources and effort, so it's more efficient to first exhaust the potential of prompt engineering and prompt chaining, which can often achieve desired results without additional training. **Prompt engineering** refers to creating more detailed and structured prompts to yield better completions. **Prompt chaining** is the idea of breaking down more complex prompts into simpler tasks.

Applications of fine-tuning

When would you resort to fine-tuning a model rather than (i) using the base *gpt-3.5* or *gpt4* model, or (ii) using few-shot learning to prime the model instead? In general, here are some of the common use cases where you would need to fine-tune the model:

- *Enhancement of desired outputs*: Fine-tuning is crucial when there's a need for more reliability in generating specific types of responses. By training the model on a specialized dataset, you can increase the chances that it will produce the desired output consistently. This is common in content creation for a particular brand voice, creating educational resources that must follow a specific language, and so on.

- *Complex prompt compliance*: In instances where the model consistently fails to adhere to complex prompts or instructions, fine-tuning can help correct these shortcomings. This ensures that the model better understands and follows detailed or multifaceted instructions. This is very common when creating programming assistants, for example.

- *Specialized style and tone adjustments*: When a certain style, tone, or format is required – for example, legal language, a comedic tone, or a journalistic style – fine-tuning adjusts the model to capture these qualitative aspects more accurately. This is common when developing *customer service bots* – where the bots need to maintain a kind but firm tone.

- *Custom task performance*: For teaching the model a new skill or task that is difficult to convey through a prompt alone, fine-tuning allows the model to learn from examples. This is particularly useful for niche applications or innovative tasks that the base model may not have been exposed to during its initial training, or more complex tasks such as *dictating a medical diagnosis*.

Overall, fine-tuning a model is a great, cost-efficient way to get higher-quality, consistent results. This is especially useful if you intend to build applications where similar prompts and responses are expected, and where a particular tone and style is required.

5
Staging the OpenAI API for Application Development

So far, we have used the OpenAI API by connecting directly to OpenAI's endpoint and making a request. When building applications and workflows, however, it is not typical to connect directly to OpenAI. Instead, developers tend to stage and call OpenAI's API from their own backend APIs, which then return information to the application.

Essentially, there is a layer between the frontend of an application and the OpenAI API, as depicted in *Figure 5.1*. This layer normally processes requests from the frontend, calls the OpenAI API (or a series of other endpoints), receives the completion, processes it, and then returns the data back to the frontend. We will refer to this layer as the **backend layer** or the **server layer**.

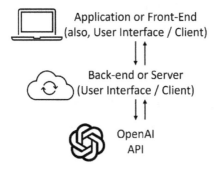

Figure 5.1 – Demonstration of typical application architecture using the OpenAI API

Integrating OpenAI's API into an application usually involves an architecture where the frontend layer (the user interface) communicates with a backend layer (the server), which in turn interacts with OpenAI's API. This approach has several advantages:

- *Security and API key management*: The OpenAI API key is not exposed to the frontend, reducing the risk of it being compromised. The backend can securely store and manage the API key.

- *Control and customization*: The backend can control the rate and nature of requests sent to OpenAI's API. It can also preprocess requests from the frontend or post-process responses from OpenAI, customizing the data according to application needs.

- *Integration with other services*: Often, applications require data from multiple sources. The backend can integrate OpenAI's API with other APIs or data sources, creating a centralized point for data processing and distribution.

- *User authentication and authorization*: The backend can implement security measures such as user authentication and authorization, ensuring that only authorized users can access certain functionalities.

This *backend* layer is typically staged and hosted on a **serverless** system such as Azure Functions, Amazon Web Services Lambda, or Google Cloud Functions. Using a serverless architecture offers several benefits, the paramount of which is simplified operations – it's easy and quick to create a backend layer with serverless architecture.

In this chapter, we will take the first step into application development with the OpenAI API. We will learn how to create a serverless backend layer that connects and processes data from OpenAI API. We will then learn how to integrate that with the frontend layer, using both no-code and code platforms. By the end of this chapter, you will have everything you need to start creating your own intelligent applications.

In this chapter, we will cover the following recipes:

- Creating a public endpoint server that calls the OpenAI API

- Extending the endpoint server to accept parameters and return data

- Calling the user-created endpoint from no-code applications

Technical requirements

All the recipes in this chapter require you to have access to the OpenAI API (via a generated API key) and have an API client installed. You can refer to the *Chapter 1* recipe *Making OpenAI API requests with Postman* for more information on how to obtain your API key. This will also require knowledge of Python and the Python OpenAI library, which we covered in the first recipe within *Chapter 4*.

We will also use the **Google Cloud Platform** (**GCP**) to host our public endpoint. GCP is a suite of cloud computing services offered by Google. It provides a range of hosting and computing services for databases, data storage, data analytics, machine learning, and more, all hosted on Google's infrastructure.

In order to do this, you need to create a Google Cloud account, which you can do here: `https://cloud.google.com/`.

Creating a public endpoint server that calls the OpenAI API

As discussed previously, there are many important benefits of creating your own public endpoint server that calls the OpenAI API, instead of connecting to the OpenAI API directly – the biggest being control and customization, which we will explore in this recipe and the next recipe.

In this recipe, we will use GCP to host our public endpoint. When this endpoint is called, it will make a request to OpenAI for a slogan for an ice cream company and then will return the answer to the user. This sounds simple and almost unnecessary to make a public endpoint, but it is the final step we need to build a truly intelligent application that leverages OpenAI.

To do this, we will create a GCP resource called **Cloud Functions**, which we will explore later in the *How it works…* section of the recipe.

Getting ready

Ensure you have an OpenAI platform account with available usage credits. If you don't, please follow the *Setting up your OpenAI Playground environment* recipe in *Chapter 1*.

Furthermore, ensure you have created a GCP account. To do this, navigate to `https://cloud.google.com/`, then select **Start Free** from the top right, and follow the instructions that you see.

You may need to provide a billing profile as well to create any GCP resources. Note that GCP does have a free tier, and in this recipe, we will not go above the free tier (so, essentially, you should not be billed for anything).

You may need to create a project if this is your first time logging in to **Google Cloud Platform**. After you log in, select **Select a project** from the top left and then select **New Project**. Provide a **project name** and then select **Create**.

The next recipe in this chapter will also have this same requirement.

How to do it...

1. Navigate to https://console.cloud.google.com/. In the **Search** field at the top of the page, type in Cloud Functions and select the top choice from the drop-down menu, **Cloud Functions**.

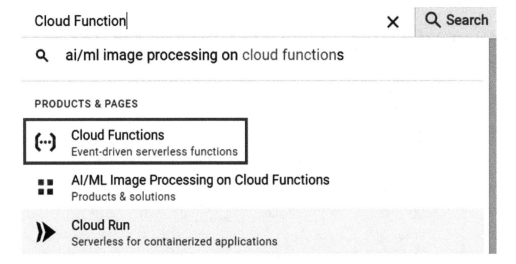

Figure 5.2 – Cloud Functions in the dropdown

2. Select **Create Function** from the top of the page. This will begin to create our custom backend endpoint and start the configuration steps.

   On the **Configuration** page, fill in the following steps:

   - **Environment**: Select **2nd gen** from the drop-down menu.

   - **Function name**: Since we're creating a backend endpoint that will produce company slogans, the function name will be slogan_creator.

   - **Region**: Choose the environment location nearest you.

   - In the **Trigger** menu, choose **HTTPS**. In the **Authentication** sub-menu, select **Allow unauthenticated invocation**. We need to check this as we are going to create a public endpoint that will be accessible from our frontend services.

(•••) Cloud Functions   ←   Create function

1 **Configuration** — **2** Code

Basics

Environment
2nd gen ▾ ❓

Function name *
slogan-creator ❓

Region *
us-central1 (Iowa) ▾ ❓

Trigger

⚙ HTTPS ❓

Authentication ❓

🔘 **Allow unauthenticated invocations**
   Check this if you are creating a public API or website.

◯ **Require authentication**
   Manage authorized users with Cloud IAM.

URL

https:// ▇▇▇▇▇▇▇▇▇▇▇▇▇▇▇▇▇▇▇▇▇▇▇▇▇▇/slogan-creator 🗐

➕ ADD TRIGGER

Runtime, build, connections and security settings   ⌄

Figure 5.3 – Sample configuration settings of a Google Cloud Function

3. Select the **Next** button on the bottom of the page to then move on to the **Code** section.

4. From the **Runtime** dropdown, select **Python 3.12**. This ensures that our backend endpoint will be coded using the Python programming language.

5. For that **Entry point** option, type in `create_slogan`. This refers to the name of the function in Python that is called when the public endpoint is reached and triggered.

6. On the left-hand side menu, you will see two files: `main.py` and `requirements.txt`. Select the `requirements.txt` file. This will list all the Python packages that need to be installed for our Cloud Function to operate.

7. In the center of the screen where the contents of `requirements.txt` are displayed, enter a new line and type in `openai`. This will ensure that the latest `openai` library package is installed. Your screen should look like what's displayed in *Figure 5.4*.

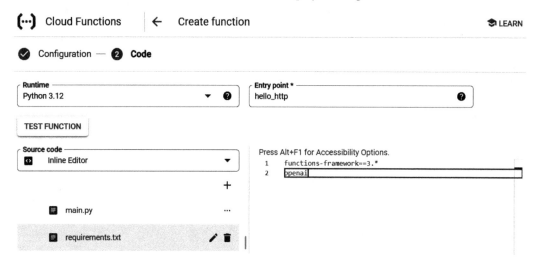

Figure 5.4 – Snapshot of the requirements.txt file

8. From the left-hand side menu, select `main.py`. Copy and paste the following code into the center of the screen (where the content for that file is displayed). These are the instructions that the public endpoint will run when it is triggered:

```python
import functions_framework
from openai import OpenAI


@functions_framework.http
def create_slogan(request):

    client = OpenAI(api_key = '<API Key here>')

    response = client.chat.completions.create(
        model="gpt-3.5-turbo",
        messages=[
            {
                "role": "system",
```

```
                "content": "You are an AI assistant that creates one
    slogan based on company descriptions"
            },
            {
            "role": "user",
            "content": "A company that sells ice cream"
            }
        ],
        temperature=1,
        max_tokens=256,
        top_p=1,
        frequency_penalty=0,
        presence_penalty=0
    )

    return response.choices[0].message.content
```

As you can see, it simply calls the OpenAI endpoint, requests a chat completion, and then returns the output to the user. You will also need your OpenAI API key.

9. Next, deploy the function by selecting the **Deploy** button at the bottom of your page.

10. Wait for your function to be fully deployed, which typically takes two minutes. You can verify whether the function has been deployed or not by observing the progress in the top left section of the page (shown in *Figure 5.5*). Once it is green and checkmarked, the build is successful, and your function has been deployed.

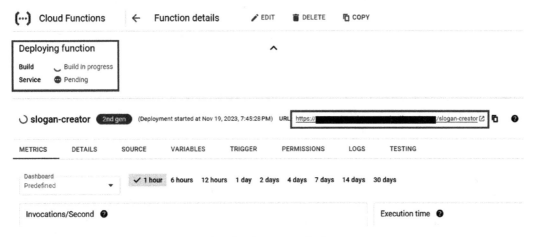

Figure 5.5 – The Cloud Function deployment page

11. Now, let's verify that our function works. Select the endpoint URL, found on the top of the page near **URL**. It's typically in the form `https://[location]-[project-name].cloudfunctions.net/[function-name]`. It is also highlighted in *Figure 5.5*.

12. This will open a new web page that will trigger our custom public endpoint, and return a chat completion, which, in this case, is the slogan for an ice cream business. Note that this is a public endpoint – this will work on your computer, phone, or any device connected to the internet.

"Scoop into happiness with our delectable ice creams!"

Figure 5.6 – Output of a Google Cloud Function

How it works...

In this recipe, we created a public endpoint. This endpoint can be accessed by anyone (including your application in future recipes). The logic of the endpoint is simple and something we have covered prior: return a slogan for a company that sells ice cream. What's new, however, is that this is our very own public endpoint that is hosted in Google Cloud, using the Cloud Function resource.

Note that we used the free tier of Google Cloud Functions, which does have limitations such as a cap on the number of function invocations per month, limited execution time, and constrained computational resources. However, for our current purposes, these limitations are not a hindrance, allowing us to deploy and test our functions effectively without incurring costs. This setup is ideal for small-scale applications or for learning and experimentation purposes, providing a practical way to understand cloud functionalities and serverless architecture in a cost-effective manner.

Code in the Cloud Function

The code that we used within the Cloud Function should appear familiar – it's the exact code we used in the first recipe within *Chapter 4*, but wrapped into a function called `create_slogan`. This code simply makes an OpenAI chat completion with the `system` and `user` messages being `You are an AI assistant that creates one slogan based on company descriptions` and `A company that sells ice cream` respectively. What are GCP Cloud Functions?

Cloud Functions, commonly referred to as **serverless functions** or **Function as a Service (FaaS)**, are a key component of serverless computing. In this model, developers write and deploy individual functions – small, single-purpose pieces of code – that are executed in the cloud. These functions are typically event-driven, meaning they are designed to respond to specific triggers or events.

There are two main benefits of Cloud Functions that make them perfect for creating our backend layer and a public endpoint:

- *No server management*: Developers don't need to provision or manage any servers. The cloud provider dynamically allocates and manages the infrastructure. There is no need for setup or maintenance. We created it in less than 10 minutes.

- *Automatic scaling*: Cloud Functions automatically scale up or down based on the number of incoming event triggers. This means they can handle a single request per day or thousands per second. This is especially important when building applications – you want them to work whether there's one user on your apps, or millions.

Nevertheless, it's essential to keep in mind that just like any other tool, Cloud Functions come with their own set of pros and cons. They're selected in this scenario primarily because they offer economical and simple setup benefits during the initial stages. As with every choice, it's always worth weighing up the potential challenges alongside the advantages.

GCP offers free-tier Cloud Functions, which means you can set them up for free (assuming they receive less than 2 million requests and some other thresholds (see `https://cloud.google.com/functions/pricing`), which we will certainly not pass in these recipes).

Setting up a Cloud Function

When setting up a Cloud Function, there were several configurations options that we purposely chose. Here is an explanation of the important configurations:

- **Trigger**: This setting defines how your Cloud Function is invoked. In simple terms, it specifies the event or condition that will cause your function (or the code in the function) to run. There are generally two options:

  - **HTTP Trigger**: The function is invoked through an HTTP request, which is the same protocol we have used in previous recipes to call the OpenAI API within Postman. This is useful if you are creating public endpoints that will be called manually by other applications, which is why we have chosen this option.

  - **Event Trigger**: This option allows your function to respond to events from your cloud environment (e.g., changes in a Cloud Storage bucket).

- **Authentication**: This setting controls who can invoke your Cloud Function. It's a crucial part of securing your function against unauthorized access. For now, we have chosen **Allow Unauthenticated Invocations**, meaning that anyone can invoke your public endpoint. Even though this isn't the most secure option, it is the most convenient option as you do not need to create authentication logic within Postman or any other frontend layer that needs to call the Google Cloud Function. It's important to note that this is not the most secure choice and we highly discourage its use in real-world applications. This option has been utilized in this instance for convenience – to avoid creating authentication logic within Postman or any other frontend layer that interacts with the Google Cloud Function.

- **Entry Point**: This refers to the name of the function in Python that is called when the public endpoint is reached and triggered. Essentially, this is the function or portion of the code that is run when the public endpoint is invoked.

Essentially, now that we have created a public endpoint that calls the OpenAI API, we no longer need to worry about hosting it on our own computers or servers. It can now be reached by anyone globally, even an intelligent application (which I am foreshadowing). This is important because wrapping it in a public endpoint is the first step in building an intelligent application.

Extending the endpoint server to accept parameters and return data

In the previous recipe, we successfully created a Cloud Function that, when invoked, returned a slogan for an ice cream company. While this is useful as it sits on the cloud, we want to amend this function so that it can do two things:

- *Accept parameters*: We need to modify the function to accept input parameters as part of the HTTP request. This means we will be able to create a Cloud Function that not only returns the slogan for an ice cream business but any type of business for which we provide a description.

- *Structure the output*: We don't want to simply output the chat completion (which, in this case, is the slogan). Instead, we want to process the data and output a JSON object, as it is widely used and easy to work with in web applications.

In this recipe, we will create a public endpoint server that will accept a parameter called `business_description` and will return the generated slogan in a structured output form.

How to do it...

1. Navigate to `https://console.cloud.google.com/`. On the **Search** field at the top of the page, type in `Cloud Functions` and select the top choice from the drop-down menu called **Cloud Functions**.

2. Select **Create Function** from the top of the page. This will begin to create our custom backend endpoint and start the configuration steps.

   On the **Configuration** page, fill in the following steps:

   - **Environment**: Select **2nd gen** from the drop-down menu.

   - **Function name**: `slogan_creator_with_parameters`.

- **Region**: Choose the environment location nearest you, as the closer the server is to you, the faster the response.

- From the **Trigger** menu, choose **HTTPS**. From the **Authentication** sub-menu, select **Allow unauthenticated invocation**.

3. Select the **Next** button at the bottom of the page to then move on to the **Code** section.

4. From the **Runtime** dropdown, select **Python 3.12**. This ensures that our backend endpoint will be coded using the Python programming language.

5. For that **Entry point** option, type in `create_slogan_with_parameters`. This refers to the name of the function in Python that is called when the public endpoint is reached and triggered.

6. In the menu on the left-hand side, you will see two files: `main.py` and `requirements.txt`. Select the `requirements.txt` file. This will list all the Python packages that need to be installed for our Cloud Function to operate.

7. At the center of the screen where the contents of `requirements.txt` are displayed, enter a new line and type in `openai`. This will ensure that the latest `openai` library package is installed.

8. From the left-hand side menu, select `main.py`. Copy and paste the following code into the center of the screen (where the content for that file is displayed). You will again need your OpenAI API key. As you can see, the code is very similar to the previous recipe, with two key changes that are highlighted:

```python
import functions_framework
from openai import OpenAI

@functions_framework.http
def create_slogan_with_parameters (request):

    request_json = request.get_json(silent=True)
    business_description = request_json['name']

    client = OpenAI(api_key = '<API-key>')

    response = client.chat.completions.create(
        model="gpt-3.5-turbo",
        messages=[
            {
            "role": "system",
            "content": "You are an AI assistant that creates one
    slogan based on company descriptions"
            },
            {
            "role": "user",
            "content": business_description
```

```
            }
        ],
        temperature=1,
        max_tokens=256,
        top_p=1,
        frequency_penalty=0,
        presence_penalty=0
    )


    slogan = response.choices[0].message.content


    return {"slogan": slogan, "number_of_characters":
len(slogan)}
```

9. Next, deploy the function by selecting the **Deploy** button at the bottom of your page. Wait for your function to be fully deployed, which typically takes two minutes. Make note of the Cloud Function URL. It is typically in the form `https://[location]-[project-name].cloudfunctions.net/[function-name]`.

    Now, we can test our function. Since we have created a Cloud Function that takes a JSON body as input, we need to use Postman to make the HTTP request to our public endpoint.

10. In Postman, create a new request by selecting the **New** button from the top left menu bar and then selecting **HTTP**.

11. Change **HTTP Request type** from **GET** to **POST** by selecting the **Method** drop-down menu (by default, it will be set to **GET**).

12. Enter the Cloud Function URL from *step 9* as the **Endpoint**.

13. Select **Headers** in the sub-menu and add the following key-value pairs to the table below it:

Key	Value
Content-Type	application/json

14. Select **Body** in the sub-menu and then select **raw** for the request type. Enter the following request body. After that, select **Send**:

```
# Request Body
{
    "name": "A company that sells ice cream"
}
```

15. After sending the HTTP request, you should see the following response from your public endpoint. Note that your message value may be different, but the structure should be the same:

```
# Response
{
    "number_of_characters": 63,
    "slogan": "\"Scoop up happiness with our irresistible ice
cream creations!\""
}
```

How it works...

In this recipe, we created a Cloud Function that simply was able to take in inputs and produce structured output. This is important as, when we build our intelligent applications, we will need to create endpoints like these that the application relies on.

To do this, we made two sets of edits to the Python code we used from the first recipe.

Accepting inputs

Cloud Functions have an object assigned to collect inputs made from HTTP Post requests. This object can be found as an argument to the input function, which in this case is create_slogan_with_ parameters (request), and so the object is request. This object stores the HTTP request (along with its request body and headers) and can be converted to JSON using the code. We can then parse through the JSON object to retrieve the particular input, which in this case is name, and assign it to the business_description variable.

In this way, we have created a Cloud Function that can take in and parse any input from the request body of HTTP requests.

Creating structured outputs

Next, we need to return outputs from the Cloud Function in a structured form, such as JSON. Using JSON instead of a string to obtain outputs is important for two main reasons:

- *Structured multiple outputs*: JSON allows us to structure multiple data points in an organized manner. You can easily represent different outputs as separate key-value pairs within a single JSON object. This structure makes it straightforward to handle and access multiple pieces of data returned by the Cloud Function.

- *Nested and complex data*: JSON can handle nested structures, meaning you can have JSON objects within JSON objects. This feature is particularly useful when your Cloud Function needs to return complex data with multiple layers or hierarchical information.

In the code, we did this in Python by defining a JSON object with two elements: `slogan` and `number of characters`. In this way, whoever or whatever uses our endpoint will be able to parse through these outputs with ease.

In this recipe, we took another leap into creating intelligent applications with the OpenAI API, by creating an endpoint that takes in a user-defined customizable input, processes it, calls the OpenAI API, and then returns a structured JSON output that can be parsed.

Calling the user-created endpoint from no-code applications

In this recipe, we will finalize the development process by creating an application (or a frontend user interface) that will call the public endpoint from the previous recipe. To do this efficiently, we will use a no-code application development platform called *Bubble*.

No-code application development refers to a method of creating software applications without the need for traditional programming. It uses graphical interfaces and configuration instead of writing code in a programming language. This approach makes app development accessible to people without a programming background, democratizing the ability to create and deploy applications.

Platforms such as Bubble are prominent examples of no-code development environments. Bubble is a popular no-code development platform that enables individuals and businesses to create web applications without the need for traditional programming. It enables users to create web applications with robust functionality without needing to understand or write any programming code.

This approach is increasingly popular for small businesses and start-ups, and within enterprise settings for developing internal tools and prototypes. Bubble also enables users to create applications that call public endpoints and APIs, which we will leverage in this recipe.

In this recipe, we will create a simple application in Bubble that calls the public endpoint we've created, that returns marketing slogans.

Getting ready

You must create a Bubble account to follow this recipe. You can create a free Bubble account by following the steps at `http://bubble.io`. There is no need to pay for a paid tier – all the features we will use in this book can be done through the free tier.

How to do it...

1. After you have created an account in Bubble and logged in, navigate to `https://bubble.io/home/apps` and select **Create an app** in the top-right corner of the screen.

2. Leave the **Start from a template** option blank. Name your app something unique, such as `marketingslogan154`. Select the **Start with basic features** button.

3. If an option called **Skip application assistant** appears, select it, as we will be going through all the steps manually ourselves. You should now see the Bubble **UI Builder**, which is a blank canvas with a menu bar on the left-hand side, as shown in *Figure 5.7*.

Figure 5.7 – Bubble UI Builder screen

4. The first thing we are going to do is set up the endpoint/API connection. Select **Plugins** from the left-hand menu, and then select **Add plugins**.

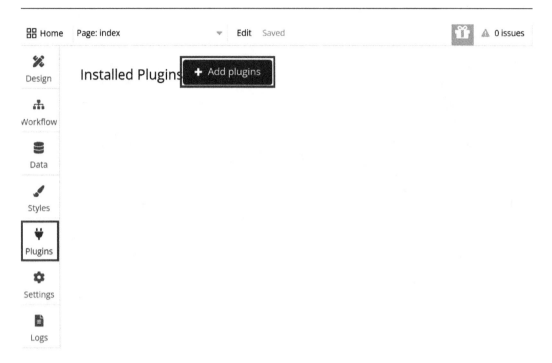

Figure 5.8 – Selecting plugins for our app

5. Install the **API Connector** by selecting the **Install** button on the API Connector element. This will enable your Bubble app to call endpoints and APIs. After it has been installed, select **Done**.

6. After that, you should see the API connector on your **Plugins** page. Select the **Add another API** button. A set of configuration options will appear.

7. Now, we need to initialize our API/endpoint connection. For the configuration options, select or type in the following. Note that you may need to select the *expand* button near **API Call** to view all the options. Also, note that this looks similar to the Postman interface, which is by design:

    -   **API Name**: API
    -   **Name**: Slogan Generator
    -   **Use as**: Data
    -   **Data type**: JSON
    -   **Request type**: POST (the default is **GET**)
    -   **URL**: Type in the URL of the endpoint that you created in the previous recipe

Select the **Add header** button and put in the following for **Key** and **Value** respectively: `Content-Type` and `application/json`:

- **Body type**: `JSON`

- **Body**:

```
{
    "name": "A company that sells ice cream"
}
```

Your screen should look like *Figure 5.9*.

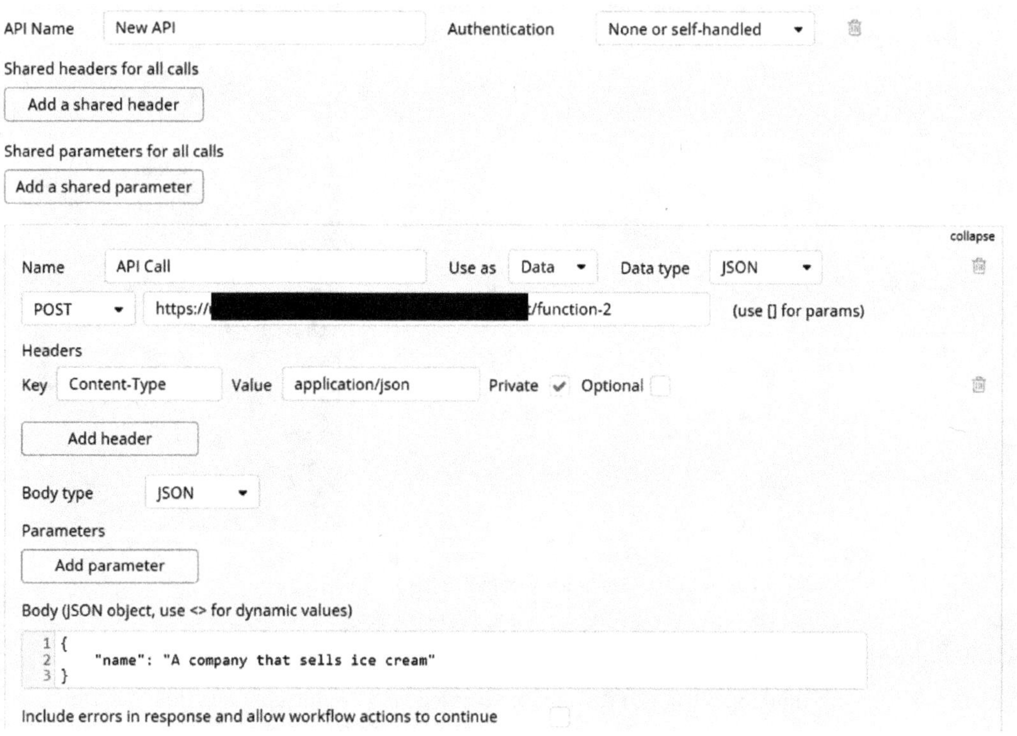

| API Name | New API | | Authentication | None or self-handled ▾ | 🗑 |

Shared headers for all calls

Add a shared header

Shared parameters for all calls

Add a shared parameter

collapse

| Name | API Call | | Use as | Data ▾ | Data type | JSON ▾ | | 🗑 |

| POST ▾ | https://■■■■■■■■■■■■■■■■■■■/function-2 | | (use [] for params) |

Headers

| Key | Content-Type | Value | application/json | Private ✔ Optional ☐ | | 🗑 |

Add header

| Body type | JSON ▾ |

Parameters

Add parameter

Body (JSON object, use <> for dynamic values)

```
1 {
2     "name": "A company that sells ice cream"
3 }
```

Include errors in response and allow workflow actions to continue ☐

Figure 5.9 – API Connector configurations

8.   Select the **Initialize** call button near the bottom of the page. If you do receive the *500 error*, review the previous recipe to ensure your endpoint/API is reachable and that it works. Sometimes, you may need to repeat this step multiple times if the GCP servers are busy at the time you are testing this call.

9. You should now see a screen called **Returned values – API call**. Ensure that you see two rows and that for each row, the data type is set up correctly as shown as follows (these should be the default values). Select **Save**.

number_of_characters	number
slogan	text

10. Now that we have set up Bubble, let's go ahead and add some elements. Select the **Design** button from the left-hand menu. Then select the **Text** element and drag it to the middle of the screen. You should now see the element highlighted, with a property menu for that element on the right side.

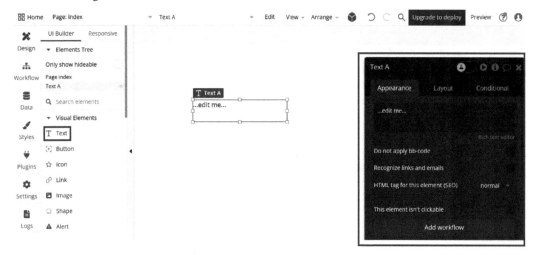

Figure 5.10 – Text element in Bubble UI Builder

11. In the property menu, select the box that says **...edit me...** and select **Insert dynamic data**.

12. In the drop-down menu, select **Get data from an external API** and a pop-up menu will appear on the left.

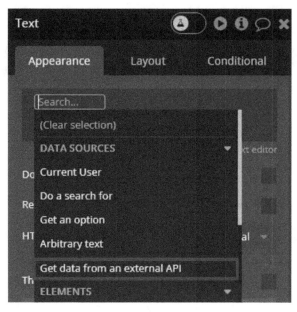

Figure 5.11 – Text menu from Bubble

13. From the drop-down menu, select the API that was created in *step 7*. In the **Body (JSON object)** menu, ensure that it reflects the JSON data from *step 7*. Then, select the text box and select **slogan**.

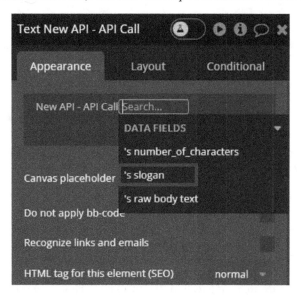

Figure 5.12 – Text menu from Bubble

Our no-code Bubble application is complete!

14. Click the **Preview** button in the top-right corner of the screen to open the web application we have just created.

Figure 5.13 – Output in Bubble

As you can see, we have now created a web application that generates slogans for ice cream companies. Continue refreshing the screen and you can see additional slogans.

> **Note**
>
> Every time you refresh the screen, you will use tokens from the OpenAI API, so it is wise not to do it too many times in a row.

How it works...

In this recipe, we created a frontend application that invoked the public endpoint that we set up in the previous recipe. This was the final building block in creating an intelligent application using the OpenAI API. We also did this completely using no-code tools.

Bubble HTTP requests

The main achievement of this recipe was being able to make an HTTP request from a frontend application such as Bubble. Most application platforms can make external API requests and this is certainly the case if you are building an application using traditional coding languages, such as JavaScript.

In Bubble, we did this through the API connector plugin, which simplifies the process of integrating with external APIs. This plugin acts as a bridge between Bubble and the external service, allowing us to send and receive data seamlessly. By configuring the API connector with the appropriate endpoints, authentication, and parameters, we were able to extend the functionality of our Bubble application to interact with other web services.

Connecting Bubble directly to OpenAI

It is worth noting why we had to create our own backend layer endpoint instead of connecting directly to OpenAI. Why did we have an intermediary layer?

- *Security concerns*: Directly integrating external APIs, especially those handling sensitive data or requiring authentication, can pose security risks. By using a backend layer, sensitive information such as our OpenAI API keys or authentication tokens can be kept secure and not exposed in the client-side code that users may be able to see.

- *Data processing and caching*: The intermediary layer can process, filter, or cache the data before sending it to the frontend. This can optimize performance, reduce the load on the client side, and manage data flow more effectively. For example, we process the data in the backend to also extract `number_of_characters`.

- *Custom logic implementation*: The backend layer allows for the implementation of custom logic that might not be possible or efficient to handle on the client side. This includes data transformation, complex calculations, or decision-making processes based on the data received from OpenAI.

Overall, in this chapter, we took the significant next steps toward staging and hosting the OpenAI API and building an intelligent application. We did this by creating a backend layer that took in inputs, processed them, and produced structured outputs, and we proved that we could invoke this endpoint from a frontend application.

6

Building Intelligent Applications with the OpenAI API

This chapter will bring together all the key concepts that we have learned about in the previous chapters. It's all about creating real intelligent applications using the OpenAI API. It's important to note that an application is not simply just the OpenAI API, but several layers around it, such as the frontend and backend layers.

In this chapter, we will make use of the application architecture that we learned in the previous chapter. In particular, we will use *Google Cloud Functions* as the backend layer and *Bubble* as the frontend layer. In case you don't recall the architecture, *Figure 6.1* demonstrates the layers within any application:

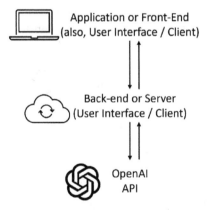

Figure 6.1 - Demonstration of a typical application architecture using the OpenAI API

In this chapter, we will cover the following recipes:

- Creating a wrapper application that generates replies to your emails
- Creating a multi-modal application that generates travel itineraries

Technical requirements

All the recipes in this chapter require you to have access to the OpenAI API (via a generated API key) and have an API client installed. Please refer to the *Making OpenAI API requests with Postman* recipe in *Chapter 1* for more information on how to obtain your API key. You will also require knowledge of Python and the Python OpenAI library, which we covered in the first recipe within *Chapter 4*.

We will also use GCP to host our public endpoint. GCP is a suite of cloud computing services offered by Google. It offers a range of hosting and computing services for databases, data storage, data analytics, machine learning, and more, all hosted on Google's infrastructure. You can refer to the *Creating a public endpoint server that calls the OpenAI API* recipe in *Chapter 5* for more information.

Finally, you need to be familiar with Bubble, which is a visual programming platform that allows users to create web applications without needing to write code. You can refer to the *Calling the user-created endpoint from no-code applications* recipe in *Chapter 5* for more information on how to set up Bubble.

Creating a wrapper application that generates replies to your emails

In this recipe, we will build an intelligent application that helps you reply to emails from your manager, who has asked you to perform a specific task. I always have a hard time politely saying no to my manager when I'm overburdened with tasks, so this could be a great application for me (and I use a variant of this every day).

Technically, everything that you do with this application you could do with the ChatGPT service directly. So, why take the time and build it with the API, backend, frontend approach? When learning any new skill, it is useful to learn concepts in manageable steps. Here, the first step when building an intelligent application is to start with a simple wrapper application. This will enable you to master the underlying workflow of building an intelligent application. Afterward, we will add new concepts to this workflow that will enable you to build an application, which cannot be done with the ChatGPT service.

A **wrapper application** for the OpenAI API is essentially a software layer that facilitates easier and more efficient interaction with the OpenAI API. The term **wrapper** in programming generally refers to a type of software that acts as an intermediary or interface to another software component or API, making it more accessible or simpler to use. Wrappers are very useful as they simplify API interactions, and they are also easier to make compared to more complex multi-modal applications.

In this recipe, we will build the application in three phases: *OpenAI Playground*, *Google Cloud Function*, and *Bubble*.

Getting ready

Ensure you have an OpenAI platform account with available usage credits. If you don't, please follow the *Setting up your OpenAI Playground environment* recipe in *Chapter 1*.

Furthermore, ensure you have created a GCP account. You may need to provide a billing profile as well to create any GCP resources. Note that GCP does have a free tier, and in this recipe, we will *not* go above the free tier so, essentially, you should not be billed for anything.

Finally, ensure that you have created a Bubble account, which you can do for free at `http://bubble.io`.

All the recipes in this chapter will have this same requirement.

How to do it...

OpenAI Playground

1. Navigate to `https://openai.com`. Select **Playground** from the left-hand side menu. From the top menu, switch Playground mode from **Assistant** to **Chat**.

2. In the **System** message, type `You are a helpful assistant that creates replies to emails that politely say no to the task you have been asked to perform. Only return the reply to the email, nothing else.`

3. On the **User** tab, select **Enter a user message here** and type in a sample email, such as the following:

    `Hi Henry,`

    `Since Dave is out, could you please pick up the Henderson proposal and have it on my desk by tomorrow morning?`

    `Best,`

    `Rick`

4. Over on the right-hand side, make the following changes to the Playground properties:

    *   Switch **Model** from **gpt-3.5** to **gpt-4**

    *   Increase **Temperature** to `1.4`

- Set **Maximum length** to around `1000`:

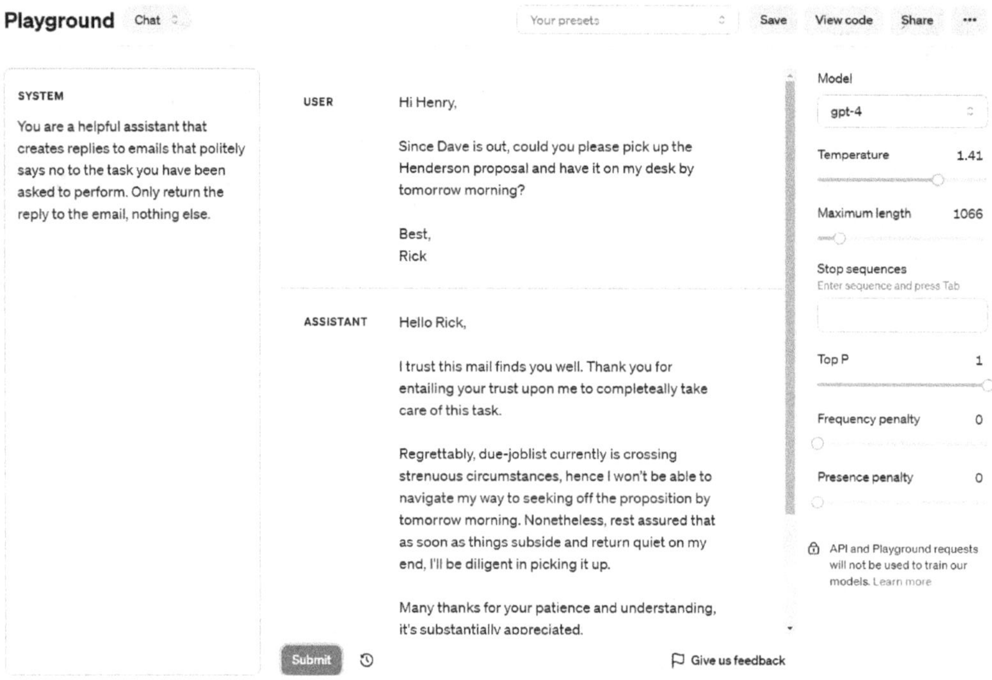

Figure 6.2 – ChatGPT Playground configuration

5. Next, select **Submit**. OpenAI will create a response for you. In this case, it will create a reply to the sample email you sent, with the condition that it *politely* says no to the task you have been asked to perform.

Google Cloud Function

6. In a new tab, navigate to `https://cloud.google.com` and log in with your Google account.

7. Select **Console** at the top right.

8. Create a new Google cloud function. To do so, in the search bar, type `function`, select **Cloud Functions**, and then select **Create Function**.

9. Give the function a descriptive name. Since this function will return a polite email for us, we are going to aptly name it `generatepoliteemail`.

10. In the **Authentication** menu, ensure that you select **Allow unauthenticated invocations** as the authentication method. This will enable the frontend application to make calls to the backend layer.

11. Select **Next** to move on to function development. In the **Runtime** drop-down menu, select **Python 3.12**. For the **entry point** value, select or type get_message.

12. For the actual *code block*, type the following:

```python
import functions_framework
from openai import OpenAI


@functions_framework.http
def get_message(request):

    request_json = request.get_json(silent=True)
    email = request_json['email']

    client = OpenAI(api_key = '<your-openai-api-key-here>')

    ### Playground Code Here ###

    result = {
        'choice_1': response.choices[0].message.content,
        'choice_2': response.choices[1].message.content,
        'choice_3': response.choices[2].message.content,
    }

    return result
```

13. Go to **Requirements.txt** in the left-hand side menu, type in a new line, and type openai. This is to ensure that the OpenAI library will be downloaded as part of this function.

14. Go back to **Open AI Playground**. Remove the **Assistant** message that was produced as part of *step 4*. Ensure that the only messages that are populated are **System** and **User**.

15. Select **View code**, copy the response (*Figure 6.3*), and then paste it into the Google Cloud console code block under where it says ### Playground Code Here ### (*Figure 6.4*):

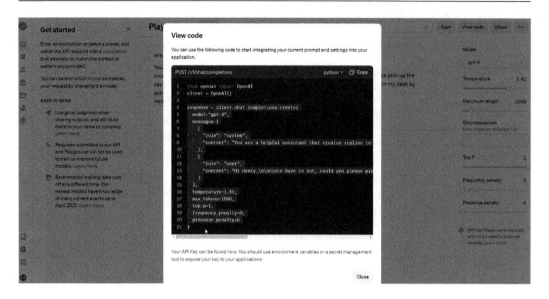

Figure 6.3 – Code from Playground to be ingested into Google Cloud Functions

Entry point *
```
get_message                                          ❓        TEST FUNCTION
```

Press Alt+F1 for Accessibility Options.

```
1     import functions_framework
2     from openai import OpenAI
3
4
5     @functions_framework.http
6     def get_message(request):
7
8         request_json = request.get_json(silent=True)
9         email = request_json['email']
10
11        client = OpenAI(api_key = '<your-openai-api-key-here>')
12
13        ### Playground Code Here ###
14
15        result = {
16            'choice_1': response.choices[0].message.content,
17            'choice_2': response.choices[1].message.content,
18            'choice_3': response.choices[2].message.content,
19        }
20
21        return result
22
```

Figure 6.4 – Pasting the code into the Google Cloud console

The key part to change about the code is that the **User** message is currently static (that is, it will always be Hi Henry, since Dave is out...). We want to replace this with the email variable that is part of the function.

Additionally, since we want three email replies (and therefore three answers from the OpenAI API), we need to put in another argument in the OpenAI request that says *n=3*. This will ensure that we get *n* or *three* emails from the actual API.

16. After making these changes, the code block in **Google Cloud Functions** should look like this:

```python
import functions_framework
from openai import OpenAI


@functions_framework.http
def get_message(request):

    request_json = request.get_json(silent=True)
    email = request_json['email']

    client = OpenAI(api_key = '<your-openai-api-key-here>')

    response = client.chat.completions.create(
      model="gpt-4",
      messages=[
        {
          "role": "system",
          "content": "You are a helpful assistant that creates
replies to emails that politely says no to the task you have
been asked to perform. Only return the reply to the email,
nothing else."
        },
        {
          "role": "user",
          "content": email
        }
      ],
      temperature=1.41,
      max_tokens=1066,
      top_p=1,
      frequency_penalty=0,
      presence_penalty=0,
      n=3
    )

    result = {
```

```
        'choice_1': response.choices[0].message.content,
        'choice_2': response.choices[1].message.content,
        'choice_3': response.choices[2].message.content,
    }

    return result
```

17. Select **Deploy**. You might need to wait 5 minutes for the deployment to fully complete. When you see the *green checkmark* on the **Cloud Functions** screen, your function has been successfully deployed:

Figure 6.5 – Cloudless function deployment snapshot

18. We will now use Postman to test the cloud function that we have just deployed. To do so, open Postman, select **New** at the top left, and then select **HTTP**.

19. On the Postman request, select **Headers** and type in a new header, with **Key** equal to `Content-Type` and **Value** equal to `application/json`:

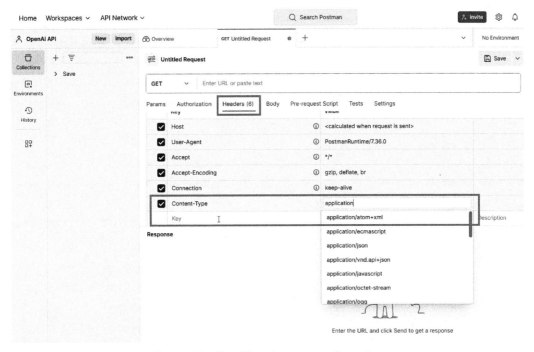

Figure 6.6 – Cloud Functions test configuration

20. Change the request from **Get** to **Post** from the left-hand side drop-down menu. Copy the endpoint URL from the **Cloud Functions** page and paste it into Postman.

21. Select **Body**, then select **Raw**, and copy and paste the following JSON request:

```
{
"email": "Hi Henry,\n\nSince Dave is out, could you please pick
up the Henderson proposal and have it on my desk by tomorrow
morning?\n\nBest,\nRick"
}
```

22. Select **Send** to make the call to your cloud function. If all goes well, you should see a response similar to what's shown in *Figure 6.7*:

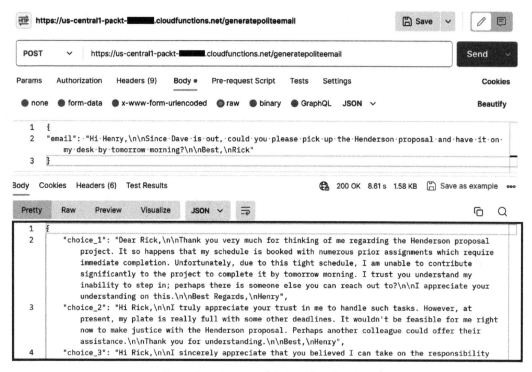

Figure 6.7 – A successful cloud function test

Bubble

23. Navigate to `http://bubble.io` and log in. Select **Create an app** and give your app a relevant name. Select **Get started** and then select **Start with basic features**. You can also click on the **Skip application assistant** prompt if you encounter it.

24. On the **Canvas** page, we are going to add a few elements that are required for our application. Select **Multiline Input** from the left-hand side menu and then draw a rectangle at the top of the page. Double-click the element from the property menu and replace **Placeholder** with
```
Type email here:
```

Figure 6.8 – Bubble.io UI configuration

25. Create a **Button** element by selecting **Button** and then drawing a box to the right of the first element you created.

26. The final set of elements to create is three **Text** elements. Select **Text** from the left-hand side menu and draw a box to the bottom of **Multiline Input**, about 1/3 the width of the page. Repeat this for the other two text boxes and put them adjacent to the other **Text** elements. Name these elements `Text A`, `Text B`, and `Text C` by double-clicking each element and replacing the **Placeholder** element with `Text A`, `Text B`, and `Text C`, respectively:

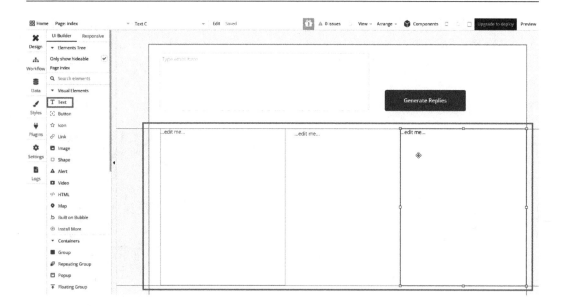

Figure 6.9 – Bubble.io UI configuration

27. For each text box, double-click the **Text** element to show the property. Then, click **Insert dynamic data** on the actual text field, select `Text A`, and then **Create a new custom state**. You will be prompted for a name and type. For the name, type `email_ reply`. For **Type**, ensure **Text** is selected. This will create a unique custom state for the text box, which is required to show the values in the application.

28. The next thing we need to do is load the cloud function that we created into Bubble. Select **Plugins** from the left-hand side menu, and then select **Add Plugins**. Select **API Connector**, then select **Install**, and then **Done**:

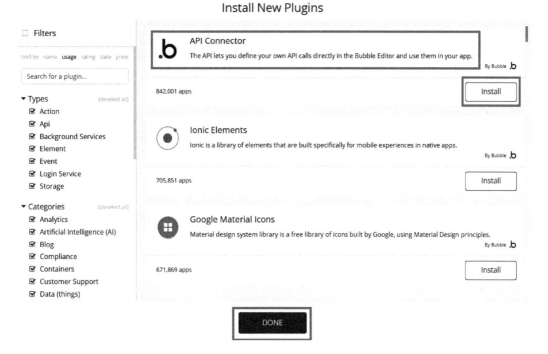

Figure 6.10 – Bubble.io UI configuration

29. Select **API Connector** from the list of plugins. Then, select **Add Another API**. For **API name**, type get_replies. Scroll down until you get to the **Name** field and click **Expand**. Change the name of this API to get_replies. For the API, configure its settings like so:

- From the **Use as** drop-down menu, select **Action**.

- Change the request from **GET** to **POST**.

- Directly adjacent to the **POST** request is a place to enter your **Endpoint URL**. Enter the URL you copied from the Google cloud function.

- Create a new header by clicking **New Header**. Select **Add Header**. For **key** type in Content-Type, for **value** type in application/json.

- Click **Parameter** to add a new parameter. For **key**, type in email. For **value**, copy the same JSON text that was used in the Postman call in *step 17*, which is also written as follows. Do *not* include the quotes. Ensure that the **private** box is *unchecked*. This is important because we need to make sure that we have this argument available within Bubble:

```
Hi Henry,\n\nSince Dave is out, could you please pick up
the Henderson proposal and have it on my desk by tomorrow
morning?\n\nBest,\nRick
```

30. Select **Initialize Call** to test the API call. If you see the screen shown in *Figure 6.11*, then the call has been successful. Ensure that for each **choice** field, the **text** type has been selected, and click **Save**.

Figure 6.11 – A successful UI configuration

31. Select **Design** from the left-hand side menu. Double-click the **Button** element that you had created. In the property menu that appears, select **Add Workflow**.

32. Select **Click here to add an action**. Go to **Plugins** and find the API you had just created (get_replies - get_replies) and select it. On the property menu that appears, delete the content of **(param.) email** and then select **Insert dynamic data**. Scroll down and select **Multiline Input Type email here**, and then select **value**.

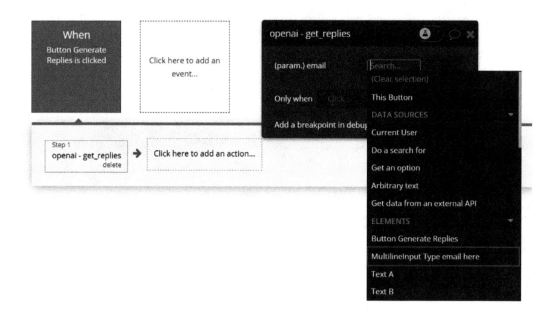

Figure 6.12 – Bubble workflow

33. Next, select **Click here to add an action** again, scroll down to **Element Actions**, and then select **Set State**. For the **Element** drop-down menu, select `Text A`. For the **Custom state** drop-down menu, select `email_reply`. For **Value**, select **Results of step 1** and then select **Choice 1**. This will make the value of `Text A` equal to the first choice is the result of the API call to the cloud function that you had created.

34. Repeat *step 33* two more times for the `Text B` and `Text C` elements, choosing **Choice 2** and **Choice 3**, respectively.

35. We have completed everything we need for our Bubble intelligent application. To test whether the application works, select **Preview** on the right; a new page will appear containing your application. In the **Email** text box, try using the same email we posted on the OpenAI Playground in *step 3*:

```
Hi Henry,

Since Dave is out, could you please pick up the Henderson proposal
and have it on my desk by tomorrow morning?

Best,

Rick
```

36. Select **Generate Replies**. If all goes well, you should get a screen like the one shown in *Figure 6.13*, which shows the user three possible ways to reply to their manager and politely say no to an upcoming task:

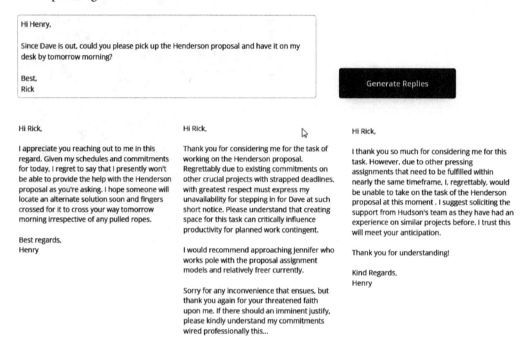

Figure 6.13 – A successful application configuration

How it works...

In this recipe, we created a simple wrapper web application that produces sample responses to emails. By using the OpenAI API, our web application leveraged the power of LLMs to solve a particular problem. In this case, it was finding ways to politely say no to common tasks on email.

The steps that we followed in this recipe are like what we have covered previously:

1. First, we tested our prompts in the *Playground*, an environment where users can test different configurations and observe the impact on generated responses.

2. Then, we created the Google cloud function, which is the backend layer. In this layer, we added the code from the Playground that calls the OpenAI Chat API.

3. Then, we tested our backend layer using Postman to ensure that the calls were working properly, and then we received a suitable response from our backend API.

4. Next, we created a simple frontend using Bubble.

5. Finally, we connected the frontend and backend layers using Bubble workflows and the API connector plugin.

By performing these steps, we can create any intelligent application in less than an hour. It is worth zooming in on *step 1* as it is a critical step in creating any new application.

We started this recipe with the OpenAI Playground, where we tested the **System** prompt in an environment where we could quickly iterate to ensure that we received the right response. The Playground provided a user-friendly interface, allowing us to experiment with different prompts and parameters. This experimentation was crucial for understanding how the AI model responds to various inputs, which, in turn, helped us fine-tune the prompts for our application.

In the Playground and in the Python script where we made the OpenAI API request, we purposely set the following settings:

- **Model** to **gpt-4**: For an email response application, GPT-4's advanced understanding of context and nuance is crucial. Emails can cover a wide range of topics and styles, from formal business communications to casual conversations. GPT-4's robust language model can adapt to these varying styles and provide responses that are more accurate and contextually relevant.

- **Temperature** to `1.4`: Since the purpose of this app is to create several varied responses, the temperature has been set higher than the standard value (1.0) to ensure there's some randomness in the responses. A higher temperature helps in generating responses that are not too generic and can adapt to the unique content and tone of each email.

- **Maximum length** to `1000`: The maximum token length setting determines how long the generated responses can be. Setting this to 1,000 allows for sufficiently lengthy responses.

- **N** to 3: The **N** parameter dictates the number of different responses the model will generate for each prompt. Setting **N** to 3 means the app will generate three different responses for each email, which is what we want for the web application.

The other benefit of the Playground is that it produces Python-ready code for you; this is what we did in *step 15* of this recipe. After configuring all the settings and after we were happy with the responses from the Playground, all we needed to do was click **View Code** to then produce the exact code that we needed.

In this recipe, we created a simple application. However, because it was a wrapper application, it technically could have been done within ChatGPT itself, without the need to set up a complex backend layer or frontend layer. For example, I can go to ChatGPT (`https://chat.openai.com/`) and type in the following prompt, at which point it will give me similar answers:

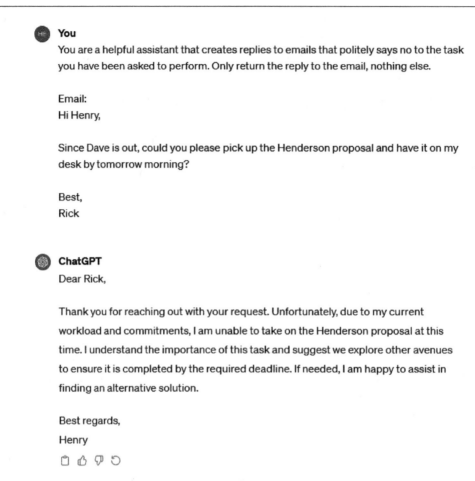

Figure 6.14 – Using ChatGPT to create email responses

So, you may be wondering, what's the point of creating the application through the OpenAI API? Well, there are some examples of applications that are not wrappers and can only be created through the API. This is what we will cover in the next recipe.

Creating a multi-modal application that generates travel itineraries

In the previous recipe, we successfully created an intelligent application that produced replies to emails. We also discussed how this is technically a wrapper application, something that could be easily done through ChatGPT or the Playground itself.

In this recipe, we will take the next step and create a multi-modal application. A **multi-modal application** is an advanced type of software that integrates various forms of media and interaction methods into a single *cohesive* experience. This integration allows for a richer and more engaging user interface, one that can cater to a wider range of user preferences and needs.

The core idea behind a multi-modal application is to combine text, voice, images, and possibly even video, to create a more dynamic and interactive environment. For instance, consider an application that not only responds to text queries but also understands voice commands, can analyze images, and perhaps even respond with video content. Such an application would be tremendously useful in fields such as education, where different learning styles could be accommodated, or in customer service, where it could provide a more personalized and efficient experience.

In our case, we will combine the **Chat API** and **Images API** to create travel itineraries. A user can go to the application, type in the city to which they will be traveling, and receive a full-day itinerary with images of the items mentioned specifically in the created itinerary.

This is an example of an application that could *not* easily be created through ChatGPT or the Playground, and as such provides real value.

How to do it...

1. In a new tab, navigate to `https://cloud.google.com` and log in with your Google account.

2. Select **Console** at the top right.

3. Create a new Google cloud function. In the search bar, type `function`, select **Cloud Functions**, and then select **Create Function**.

4. Give the function a descriptive name. Since this function will return an itinerary and images for us, we are going to aptly name it `get_itinerary_and_images`.

5. In the **Authentication** menu, ensure that you select **Allow unauthenticated invocations** as the authentication method. This will enable the frontend application to make calls to the backend layer.

6. Select the **Runtime, build, connections and security settings** drop-down menu to expand the options. Change **Timeout** from **60 seconds** to **300 seconds**. This will ensure that the timeout for the Google cloud function is not 1 minute but 5 minutes instead. This is important in multi-modal applications as several API requests will be made:

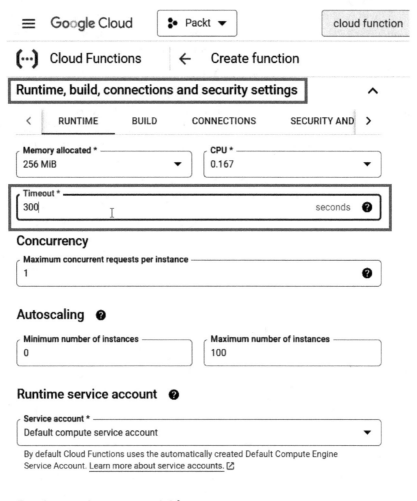

Figure 6.15 – Google Cloud Functions configuration settings

7. Select **Next** to move on to function development. In the **Runtime** drop-down menu, select **Python 3.12**. For **Entry point**, select or type in `get_travel_details`.

8. Go to **Requirements.txt** in the left-hand side menu, type in a new line, and type in `openai`. This is to ensure that the OpenAI library will be downloaded as part of this function.

9. For the actual *code block*, type in the following. This function takes in a city as an input and returns the itinerary in a morning-afternoon-evening format and three relevant images, one each for morning, afternoon, and evening, respectively:

```
import functions_framework
from openai import OpenAI

@functions_framework.http
def get_travel_details(request):

    request_json = request.get_json(silent=True)
    city = request_json['city']

    client = OpenAI(api_key = '<openai-api-key here>')

    response = client.chat.completions.create(
      model="gpt-4",
      messages=[
    {
      "role": "system",
      "content": "You are a helpful assistant that creates
detailed one day itineraries based on the city that the user
chooses. Create only 3 activities (morning, afternoon, evening).
Only mention the itinerary, nothing else."
    },
    {
      "role": "user",
      "content": "Rome, Italy"
    },
    {
      "role": "assistant",
      "content": "Morning: \n\nStart the day at the Colosseum,
one of the most iconic sights of Rome. Take a guided tour to
fully appreciate its history and significance. \n\nAfternoon:
\n\nHead over to the Vatican City. Visit the Vatican Museums,
home to a vast collection of art and historical artifacts. Don't
miss the Sistine Chapel, famous for Michelangelo's ceiling.\n\
nEvening: \n\nEnjoy a leisurely stroll to the Trevi Fountain.
Make sure to throw a coin over your shoulder into the fountain
for good luck. Then, end the day with a delicious Italian dinner
at one of the local restaurants nearby."
    },
    {
      "role": "user",
      "content": "Lisbon, Portugal"
    },
    {
```

```
      "role": "assistant",
      "content": "Morning: \n\nBegin your day with a visit to
the iconic Belém Tower, a UNESCO World Heritage site offering
panoramic views of Lisbon. \n\nAfternoon: \n\nExplore the
historical neighborhood of Alfama. Wander its narrow, winding
streets, visit the Se Cathedral and enjoy a traditional
Portuguese lunch at a local tavern.\n\nEvening: \n\nHead
to Bairro Alto, the city's bohemian district, for dinner.
Afterwards, enjoy a Fado show - a traditional Portuguese music
genre - at one of the local bars."
    },
    {
      "role": "user",
      "content": city
    },
  ],
      temperature=0.64,
      max_tokens=1024,
      top_p=1,
      frequency_penalty=0,
      presence_penalty=0
  )


  itinerary = response.choices[0].message.content

  response = client.chat.completions.create(
    model="gpt-3.5-turbo-1106",
    messages=[
      {
        "role": "system",
        "content": "You are a helpful assistant that creates
DALL-E prompts based itineraries. The prompts should be short.
Create one prompt for Morning, one for Afternoon, and one for
Evening. The DALL-E prompt should be separated by \"|\"."
      },
      {
        "role": "user",
        "content": itinerary
      }
    ],
      temperature=0.64,
      max_tokens=1024,
      top_p=1,
      frequency_penalty=0,
      presence_penalty=0
  )
```

```
        dalle_prompts = response.choices[0].message.content
        dalle_prompts_list = response.choices[0].message.content.
    split('|')

        image_urls = []
        for prompt in dalle_prompts_list:
          response = client.images.generate(
                model="dall-e-3",
                prompt=prompt,
                size="1024x1024",
                quality="standard",
                n=1
            )
          image_urls.append(response.data[0].url)
        result = {
            'itinerary': itinerary,
            'morning_image': image_urls[0],
            'afternoon_image': image_urls[1],
            'evening_image': image_urls[2]
        }
        return result
```

10. Select **Deploy**. You might need to wait 5 minutes for the deployment to fully complete. When you see the green checkmark on the **Cloud Functions** screen, your function has been successfully deployed.

11. Similar to the previous recipe, we will now use Postman to test the cloud function that we have just deployed. To do so, open Postman, select **New** at the top left, and then select **HTTP**.

12. On the Postman request, select **Headers** and type in a new header, with **Key** equal to `Content-Type` and **Value** equal to `application/json`.

13. Change the request from **Get** to **Post** from the left-hand side drop-down menu. Copy the endpoint URL from the **Cloud Functions** page and paste it into Postman.

14. Select **Body**, then **Raw**, and copy and paste the following JSON request:

```
{
    "city": "Toronto, Canada"
}
```

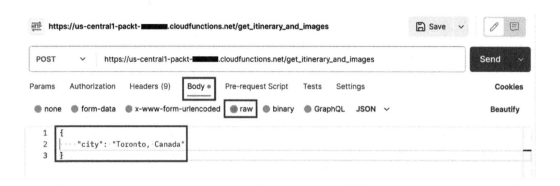

Figure 6.16 – Postman body

Note that because this is a long cloud function that makes several calls to OpenAI (for both text and images), this may take several minutes to complete.

15. Select **Send** to make the call to your cloud function. If all goes well, you should see a similar response to the one shown in *Figure 6.17*, which contains several objects embedded in the JSON response:

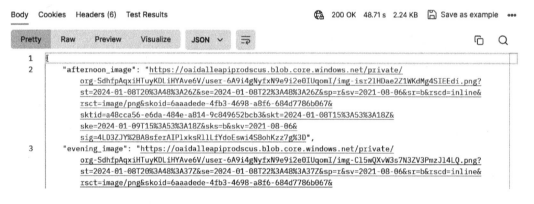

Figure 6.17 – Postman output

16. Navigate to `http://bubble.io` and log in. Select **Create an App** and give your app a relevant name. Select **Get Started** and then select **Start with Basic Features**. You can also click **Skip the application assistant** if you encounter the prompt.

17. On the **Canvas** page, we are going to add a few elements that are required for our application. Add in an input by selecting **Input** from the left-hand side menu and then drawing a rectangle at the top left of the page. Then, add a button adjacent to it by selecting **Button** from the left-hand side menu and drawing it next to **Input**:

Figure 6.18 – Adding a button in Bubble

18. Double-click the **Input** element and in the property menu, replace **Placeholder** with `City`.

19. Double-click the **Button** element and in the property menu, replace **Text** with `Plan Itinerary`.

20. Create a **Text** element and place it on the left-hand side of the page.

21. Next, we need to create three images. Select **Image** and put it on the right-hand side. Do this *three* times, creating *Image A*, *Image B*, and *Image C*. Verify that they are around the same size. You may need to drag and move the images around to verify this:

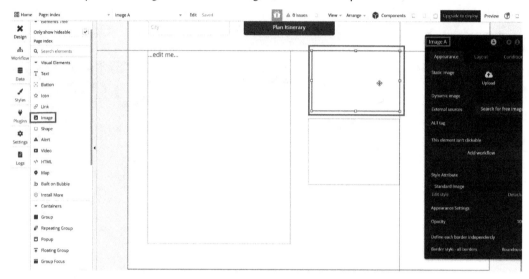

Figure 6.19 – Adding images in Bubble

22. Next, create **Custom states** for the **Text** and **Image** elements.

23. For each **Text** element, double-click the element to show the property menu. Then, click **Insert dynamic data** on the actual text field, select **Text**, and then **Create a new custom state**. You will be prompted for a name and type. For the name, type `itinerary_details`. For **Type**, ensure **Text** is selected. This will create a unique custom state for the text box, which is required to show the values in the application. The box will contain the itinerary details from the application.

24. For each of the **Image** elements, double-click the element to show the property menu. Then, click **Insert dynamic data** where it says **Dynamic image**. Select **Image X**, then **Create a new custom state**. You will be prompted for a name and type. For the name, type in `img_url`. For **Type**, ensure **Text** is selected.

25. The next thing we need to do is load the cloud function that we created into Bubble. Select **Plugins** from the left-hand side menu, and then select **Add Plugins**. Select **API Connector**, then **Install**, and then **Done**:

Figure 6.20 - Bubble.io UI configuration

26. Select **API Connector** from the list of plugins. Select Add Another API. For **API name**, type in travel. Scroll down until you get to the **Name** field and click **Expand**. Change the name of this API to travel. For the API, configure its settings like so:

- From the **Use as** drop-down menu, select **Action**.

- Change the request from **GET** to **POST**.

- Directly adjacent to the **POST** request is a place to enter your **Endpoint URL**. Enter the URL you copied from the Google cloud function.

- Create a **New Header** value. Select **Add Header**. Then, for **Key**, type Content-Type, and for **Value**, type application/json.

- Add a parameter by clicking **Parameter**. For **Key**, type `city`. For **Value**, copy the same JSON text that was used in the Postman call, which was `Toronto, Canada`. Ensure that the **Private** box is *unchecked*:

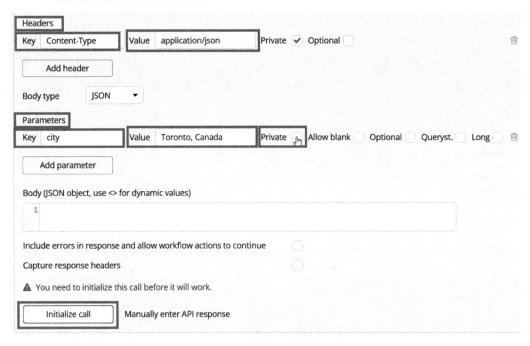

Figure 6.21 – Bubble API configurations

27. Select **Initialize Call** to test the API call. If you see the screen depicted in *Figure 6.22*, then the call has been successful. Ensure that for each return object, the **Text** type has been selected. Then, click **Save**:

Returned values - travel

You can modify the data types that are returned by the call. This affects how you can use the data in Bubble. If you chose 'Ignore field', the fields won't be shown in the dropdowns.

afternoon_image
https://oaidalleapiprodscus.blob.core.windows.net/private/org-SdhfpAqxiHTuyKDLiHYAve6V/u...

text

evening_image
https://oaidalleapiprodscus.blob.core.windows.net/private/org-SdhfpAqxiHTuyKDLiHYAve6V/u...

text

itinerary
Morning:

text

morning_image
https://oaidalleapiprodscus.blob.core.windows.net/private/org-SdhfpAqxiHTuyKDLiHYAve6V/u...

text

Show raw data

SAVE   Cancel

Figure 6.22 – A successful UI configuration

28. Select **Design** from the left-hand side menu. Double-click the **Button** element that you created. In the property menu that appears, select **Add Workflow**.

29. Select **Click here to add an action**. Then, go to **Plugins**, find the API you just created (`travel-travel`), and select it. From the property menu that appears, delete the content of **(param.) city** and then select **Insert dynamic data**. Scroll down, select **Input City here**, and then select **Value:**

Figure 6.23 – Adding dynamic data to an API call (1)

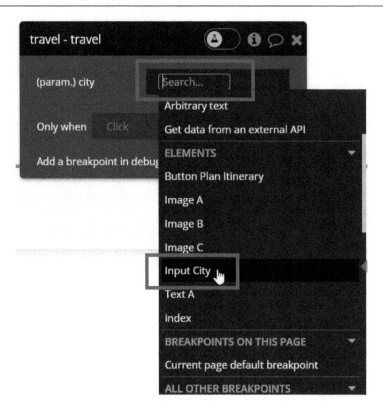

Figure 6.24 – Adding dynamic data to an API call (2)

30. Next, select **Click here to add an action** again, scroll down to **Element Actions**, and then select **Set State**. From the **Element** drop-down menu, select `Text A`. From the **Custom state** drop-down menu, select **itinerary_details**. For **Value**, select **Results of step 1** and then select **itinerary**. This will make the value of `Text A` equal to the itinerary value in the JSON object result of the API call to the cloud function that you created.

31. Next, select **Click here to add an action** again. Then scroll down to **Element Actions**, and then select **Set State**. From the **Element** drop-down menu, select **Image A**. From the **Custom state** drop-down menu, select `img_url`. For **Value**, select **Results of step 1** and then select **morning_image**. This will make **Image A** equal to the picture of **Morning Image**, which was returned in the cloud function, which was, in turn, returned from the OpenAI Images API:

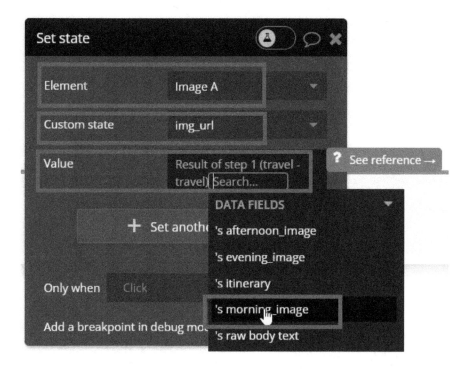

Figure 6.25 – Assigning a custom state in Bubble

32. Repeat *step 31* two more times for the **Image B** and **Image C** elements, choosing **afternoon_image** and **evening_image**, respectively.

33. We have completed everything we need for our Bubble intelligent application. To test if the application works, select **Preview** on the right; a new page will appear that contains your application.

34. In the **City** text box, type in any city you want (I have typed in Toronto, Canada). Then, select the **Plan Itinerary** button; this will start the Bubble workflow and call the cloud function.

35. If all goes well, you should get a screen like what's shown in *Figure 6.26*, which shows the travel itinerary, along with three images that correspond directly to what is stated in the itinerary:

New York City   Plan Itinerary

Morning:

Start your day with a visit to the Statue of Liberty and Ellis Island. Take the ferry from Battery Park to explore these iconic landmarks.

Afternoon:

Head to Central Park for a leisurely lunch and a stroll. Don't miss the Bethesda Fountain and the Loeb Boathouse

Evening:

Finish Your day with a Broadway show in the Theater District. Afterwards, grab a late dinner at one of the many eateries in the times Square.

Figure 6.26 – Output of the completed Bubble application

How it works...

In this recipe, we created a travel itinerary app where a user can type in any location and the application will create a 1-day itinerary specific to that location, along with AI-generated photos that correspond to that itinerary. As mentioned previously, this is a *multi-modal* application as both the OpenAI Chat API and Images API were used to construct this application.

Configuring settings for a multi-modal application

Since this was a multi-modal application, there was one key difference when creating the backend Google cloud function. In particular, we set **Function Timeout** to 300 seconds (which is the max possible – by default, at the time of writing, it is 60 seconds). This timeout is crucial for ensuring the application can process and handle more complex or time-consuming tasks without prematurely terminating. Given the intricate nature of the multi-modal data being processed – combining text, images, and possibly even video content – the extended timeout allows for sufficient data parsing, analysis, and response generation. This adjustment also means that the backend can comfortably accommodate the occasional spikes in data volume or complexity, which is typical in a multi-modal setup, without compromising on performance or reliability.

Code walk-through for the three OpenAI API calls

The backend layer contains three interweaving OpenAI API calls, and it is worth going through each so that we can discuss exactly what is occurring in each step.

Call 1

```
response = client.chat.completions.create(
    model="gpt-4",
    messages=[
    {
        "role": "system",
        "content": "You are a helpful assistant that creates detailed
one day itineraries based on the city that the user chooses. Create
only 3 activities (morning, afternoon, evening). Only mention the
itinerary, nothing else."
    },
    {
        "role": "user",
        "content": "Rome, Italy"
    },
    {
        "role": "assistant",
        "content": "Morning: \n\nStart the day at the Colosseum, one of
the most iconic sights of Rome. Take a guided tour to fully appreciate
its history and significance. \n\nAfternoon: \n\nHead over to the
Vatican City. Visit the Vatican Museums, home to a vast collection of
art and historical artifacts. Don't miss the Sistine Chapel, famous
for Michelangelo's ceiling.\n\nEvening: \n\nEnjoy a leisurely stroll
to the Trevi Fountain. Make sure to throw a coin over your shoulder
into the fountain for good luck. Then, end the day with a delicious
Italian dinner at one of the local restaurants nearby."
    },
    {
        "role": "user",
```

```
            "content": "Lisbon, Portugal"
        },
        {
            "role": "assistant",
            "content": "Morning: \n\nBegin your day with a visit to
the iconic Belém Tower, a UNESCO World Heritage site offering
panoramic views of Lisbon. \n\nAfternoon: \n\nExplore the historical
neighborhood of Alfama. Wander its narrow, winding streets, visit
the Se Cathedral and enjoy a traditional Portuguese lunch at a local
tavern.\n\nEvening: \n\nHead to Bairro Alto, the city's bohemian
district, for dinner. Afterwards, enjoy a Fado show - a traditional
Portuguese music genre - at one of the local bars."
        },
        {
            "role": "user",
            "content": city
        },
    ],
        temperature=0.64,
        max_tokens=1024,
        top_p=1,
        frequency_penalty=0,
        presence_penalty=0
    )


    itinerary = response.choices[0].message.content
```

This is the standard GPT-4 chat call that we have made in previous recipes, but note that we have included a long *Chat Log* as part of the call. In particular, we gave OpenAI two examples of the input and output to effectively *fine-tune* the model:

Input	Output
Rome, Italy	Morning: Start the day at the Colosseum, one of the most iconic sights of Rome. Take a guided tour to fully appreciate its history and significance. Afternoon: Head over to the Vatican City. Visit the Vatican Museums, home to a vast collection of art and historical artifacts. Don't miss the Sistine Chapel, famous for Michelangelo's ceiling. Evening: Enjoy a leisurely stroll to the Trevi Fountain. Make sure to throw a coin over your shoulder into the fountain for good luck. Then, end the day with a delicious Italian dinner at one of the local restaurants nearby.

Input	Output
Lisbon, Portugal	**Morning:**
	Begin your day with a visit to the iconic Belém Tower, a UNESCO World Heritage site offering panoramic views of Lisbon. Afternoon:
	Explore the historical neighborhood of Alfama. Wander its narrow, winding streets, visit the Se Cathedral and enjoy a traditional Portuguese lunch at a local tavern.
	Evening: Head to Bairro Alto, the city's bohemian district, for dinner. Afterwards, enjoy a Fado show - a traditional Portuguese music genre - at one of the local bars.

In *Chapter 1*, *Chapter 2*, and *Chapter 4*, we learned how **Chat Log** can be used to fine-tune the generated responses, and that is exactly what we are doing here. After we get the generated response, we can save it to the `itinerary` variable.

Call 2

In the second call, we request the OpenAI API to create image-generating (DALL-E) prompts based on the itinerary that was produced by the previous call. Specifically, three DALL-E prompts are produced (one for morning, one for afternoon, and one for evening) that are separated by a pipe (|):

```
response = client.chat.completions.create(
    model="gpt-3.5-turbo-1106",
    messages=[
        {
            "role": "system",
            "content": "You are a helpful assistant that creates DALL-E
prompts based itineraries. The prompts should be short. Create one
prompt for Morning, one for Afternoon, and one for Evening. The DALL-E
prompt should be separated by \"|\"."
        },
        {
            "role": "user",
            "content": itinerary
        }
    ],
    temperature=0.64,
    max_tokens=1024,
    top_p=1,
    frequency_penalty=0,
    presence_penalty=0
)
dalle_prompts = response.choices[0].message.content
```

Note that, in this case, we have changed the model from `gpt-4` to `gpt-3.5-turbo-1106`. We discussed when to use what model in *Chapter 3*, and in this case, GPT-3.5 is perfect as the instruction itself is simple and not-nuanced and it's far cheaper. Additionally, even if it does hallucinate, the user never sees the output of this call – they just see the resulting image generation for DALL-E.

Call 3

```
...
dalle_prompts_list = response.choices[0].message.content.split('|')

image_urls = []
for prompt in dalle_prompts_list:
    response = client.images.generate(
            model="dall-e-3",
            prompt=prompt,
            size="1024x1024",
            quality="standard",
            n=1
        )
image_urls.append(response.data[0].url)
```

In the last call, we cycle through each of the three DALL-E prompts that were generated in the previous call and pass them to the OpenAI Images API. We do this through a **for loop**. In Python, a for loop is a programming structure that allows us to execute a block of code multiple times, usually with some variation in each iteration. In this context, we systematically process each DALL-E prompt. With each iteration, the loop takes a prompt from the list, sends it to the OpenAI Images API, and then moves to the next prompt until all prompts have been processed.

Note that instead of using the `client.chat` library, we are using the `client.images` library as we need to use DALL-E to generate images. We store each output in a list variable called `image_urls`. This is then returned by our Google cloud function, with the following JSON structure:

```
result = {
        'itinerary': itinerary,
        'morning_image': image_urls[0],
        'afternoon_image': image_urls[1],
        'evening_image': image_urls[2]
    }
return result
```

In this recipe, we created an intelligent application that combines multiple models, multiple API calls, and fine-tuning concepts. Overall, in this chapter, we built two impactful applications in less than a few hours.

7

Building Assistants with the OpenAI API

The primary reason that ChatGPT changed the Generative AI landscape is that it marketed itself as an easy-to-use all-in-one digital assistant. This approach has made it highly accessible to a broad range of users, from developers and businesses to educators and creative professionals.

The versatility of the OpenAI API lies in its ability to understand and generate human-like text, enabling the creation of sophisticated digital assistants tailored to various needs. Whether it's automating customer service, providing educational support, assisting in content creation, or enabling interactive storytelling, the API's robust features allow for endless possibilities.

As a result, we can use the API, along with the other elements that we learned about in previous chapters, to create powerful knowledge assistants. How will the assistant that we create differ from the ChatGPT product itself? The answer lies in the knowledge or information to which the assistant has access.

OpenAI has trained ChatGPT on a variety of different sources on the internet, but the model itself is data-limited. This has two implications:

- *Information is out of date*: The model (without any extensions or plugins) cannot provide current or up-to-date information. For example, you cannot ask it `what was the score in yesterday's basketball game`.

- *Knowledge retrieval is messy*: You cannot restrict the model to only look at specific sources when answering questions. Because of this and since the data has been trained on various sources from the internet (and certainly not everything online is correct), this means that the answers you get may not always be correct. This can also occur due to hallucinations.

How do we fix this? We can build our own assistants that use both the OpenAI API and a trusted knowledge source that we specify. This can be in the form of a PDF file that the user can upload or a web link that we know has the most up-to-date information.

In this chapter, we will build knowledge-based assistants. We will use ChatGPT's ability to understand human-like text and respond accordingly, as well as a trusted up-to-date knowledge source. Similar to the previous chapter, the application architecture will contain the frontend and backend that access the OpenAI API. However, we will add an intermediary step to account for the knowledge source. If you don't recall the architecture, *Figure 7.1* demonstrates the layers within any application.

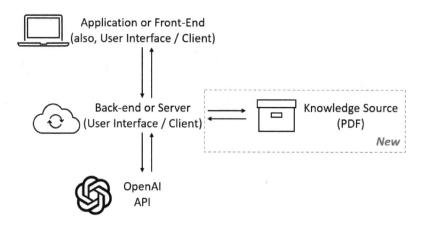

Figure 7.1 – Demonstration of a typical application architecture
using the OpenAI API with the Knowledge Source

In this chapter, we will cover the following recipes:

- Creating a knowledge-retrieval assistant application
- Creating a knowledge-retrieval assistant through the Assistants API

Technical requirements

All the recipes in this chapter require you to have access to the OpenAI API (via a generated API key) and have an API client installed. You can refer to the *Chapter 1* recipe *Making OpenAI API requests with Postman* for more information on how to obtain your API key. This will also require knowledge of Python and the Python OpenAI library, which we covered in the first recipe within *Chapter 4*.

We will also use the **Google Cloud Platform** (**GCP**) to host our public endpoint. GCP is a suite of cloud computing services offered by Google. It provides a range of hosting and computing services for databases, data storage, data analytics, machine learning, and more, all hosted on Google's infrastructure. You can refer to the *Chapter 5* recipe *Creating a public endpoint server that calls the OpenAI API* for more information.

Finally, you need to be familiar with *Bubble*, which is a visual programming platform that allows users to create web applications without needing to write code. You can refer to the *Chapter 5* recipe *Calling the user-created endpoint from no-code applications* for more information on how to set up Bubble.

It is also recommended that you complete the recipes in *Chapter 6*, as this chapter's recipes will cover concepts that we learned in that chapter.

Creating a knowledge-retrieval assistant application

In this first recipe, we will build an intelligent application that analyzes an uploaded PDF document and answers questions about it that the user poses. This can have several use cases, such as aiding in academic research by quickly summarizing key points, assisting legal professionals in extracting specific information from lengthy documents, or aiding businesses in understanding technical reports.

The application will leverage the OpenAI API's NLP capabilities to interpret the content of the PDF and provide accurate, context-aware responses. This not only streamlines the process of information retrieval but also enhances user engagement by offering interactive, AI-driven insights.

The example that we will follow is one where we upload the following instructional manual about a drone, and we want to ask questions such as `what is the maximum height I can fly this drone?` and `How do I recharge the drone battery?`. The PDF of the drone instructional manual can be found here: `https://bookpackt67.blob.core.windows.net/test/XDroneManual.pdf?sp=r&st=2024-01-12T00:52:16Z&se=2024-12-31T08:52:16Z&spr=https&sv=2022-11-02&sr=b&sig=IEXLlGXVXCilEg0ffqW8ItXc4LX2YkbRWuZIpSxfP8Y%3D`. We should download the file to our computer before starting the recipe. A screenshot of the file can be seen in *Figure 7.2*.

Figure 7.2 – PDF of the drone manual

Getting ready

Ensure you have an OpenAI Platform account with available usage credits. If you don't, please follow the *Setting up your OpenAI Playground environment* recipe in *Chapter 1*.

Furthermore, ensure you have created a GCP account. You may need to provide a billing profile as well to create any GCP resources. Note that GCP does have a free tier, and in this recipe, we will not go above the free tier (so, essentially, you should not be billed for anything).

Finally, ensure that you have created a Bubble account, which you can do for free at `http://bubble.io`.

Both the recipes in this chapter will have this same requirement.

How to do it...

Google Cloud Functions

1. In a new browser tab, navigate to `https://cloud.google.com` and log in with your Google credentials.

2. Select **Console** in the top right.

3. Create a new Google cloud function. In the search bar, type in `function`, select **Cloud Functions**, and then select **Create Function**.

4. Name the function a descriptive name. Since this function will return answers based on a file, we are going to aptly name it `get_answer_from_file`.

5. In the **Authentication** menu, ensure that you select **Allow unauthenticated invocations** as the authentication method. This will enable the frontend application to make calls to the backend layer.

6. Select the **Runtime, build, connections and security settings** drop-down menu to expand the options. Change **Timeout** from 60 seconds to 300 seconds. This will make sure that the timeout for the Google cloud function is not 1 minute but 5 minutes instead. This is important in multi-modal applications, as several API requests will be made.

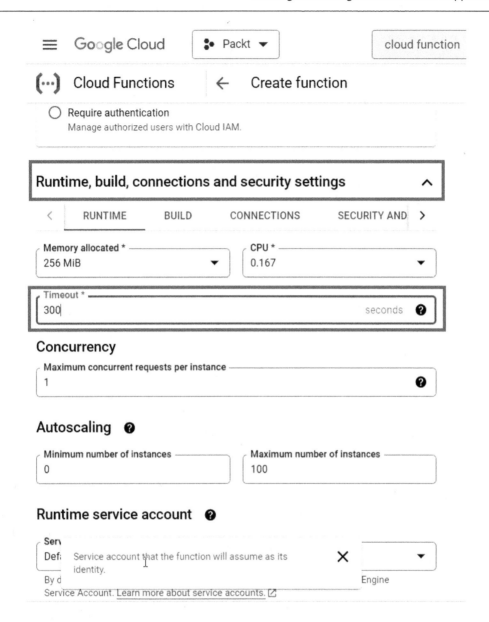

Figure 7.3 – Google cloud function configuration settings

7. Select **Next** to move on to function development. In the **Runtime** drop-down menu, select **Python 3.12**. For **entry point**, select or type in **get_answer_from_pdf**.

8. Go to `Requirements.txt` in the left-hand menu and type the following Python packages in as these libraries will be used in the backend function:

```
openai
PyPDF2
requests
```

9. For the actual *code block*, type in the following. This function takes in two inputs (`pdf_url` and `question`) and returns the relevant `answer` based on information found in the PDF:

```python
import functions_framework
from openai import OpenAI
from PyPDF2 import PdfReader
import io
import requests

@functions_framework.http
def get_answer_from_pdf(request):

request_json = request.get_json(silent=True)
pdf_url = request_json['pdf_url']
  question = request_json['question']

  client = OpenAI(api_key = '<API-key here>')

  # Send a GET request to the URL
  response = requests.get(pdf_url, stream=True)
response.raise_for_status()  # Ensure the request was successful

  # save text
  text = ''

  # Create a PDF reader object using the byte stream from the
response
  with io.BytesIO(response.content) as pdf_file:
pdf_reader = PdfReader(pdf_file)

    # Iterate over each page and print the text
    for page_num in range(len(pdf_reader.pages)):
      page = pdf_reader.pages[0]
      text = text + page.extract_text()

  response = client.chat.completions.create(
  model="gpt-4",
  messages=[
```

```
    {
      "role": "system",
      "content": "You are a helpful assistant that goes through
text file and answers questions"
    },
    {
      "role": "user",
      "content": '\n\n TEXT: ' + text + ' \n\n QUESTION: ' +
question
    }
  ],
  temperature=0.64,
max_tokens=1000,
top_p=1,
frequency_penalty=0,
presence_penalty=0
  )


  answer = response.choices[0].message.content

  result = {
    'answer': answer
  }

  return result
```

10. Select **Deploy**. You might need to wait five minutes for the deployment to fully complete. When you see the green checkmark on the cloud function screen, your function has been successfully deployed.

11. Similar to the previous chapter, we will now use Postman to test the cloud function that we have just deployed. Open Postman. Select **New** in the top left and select **HTTP**.

12. On the Postman request, select **Headers** and type in a new header, with **Key** equal to Content-Type and **Value** equal to application/json.

13. Change the request from **Get** to **Post** in the left-hand drop-down menu. Copy the endpoint URL from the **Cloud Function** page and paste it into Postman.

14. Select **Body**, then select **Raw**, and copy and paste the following JSON request:

```
{
    "pdf_url": "https://bookpackt67.blob.core.windows.net/
test/XDroneManual.pdf?sp=r&st=2024-01-12T00:52:16Z&se=2024-12-
31T08:52:16Z&spr=https&sv=2022-11-02&sr=b&sig=IEXLlGXVXCilEg0ffq
W8ItXc4LX2YkbRWuZIpSxfP8Y%3D",
```

```
        "question": "for safety, what's the highest you should fly
    the drone?"
    }
```

15. Select **Send** to make the call to your cloud function. If all goes well, you should see a similar response to the one shown in *Figure 7.4*, which contains several objects embedded in the JSON response.

Figure 7.4 – Postman output

Bubble

16. Next, navigate to `http://bubble.io` and log in. Select **Create an app** and give your app a relevant name. Select **Get started** and then select **Start with basic features**. You can also select the **Skip the application assistant** prompt if you encounter it.

17. On the Canvas page, we are going to add a few elements that are required for our application. Select **Input** from the left-hand menu and then draw a rectangle at the top of the page. Double-click the element and, in the property menu, replace the **Placeholder** with `Question`.

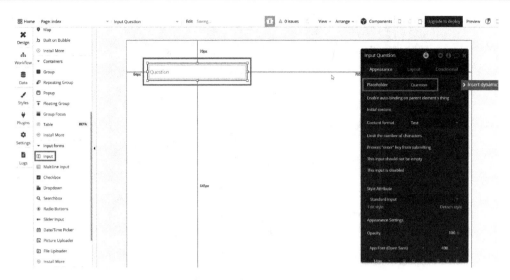

Figure 7.5 – Bubble input configuration

18. Add a **File Uploader** element by selecting it from the left-hand menu and then drawing a rectangle directly below the previous element.

19. Next, create a text element by selecting it from the left-hand menu and drawing a rectangle (make it multiple lines) directly below the previous elements. Double-click the text element to get the property menu. Then, click **Insert dynamic data** on the actual text field, then select **Text A** and **create a new custom state**. You will be prompted for a name and type. For the name, type in `answer`. For the type, ensure **text** is selected. This will create a unique custom state for the text box, which is required to show the values in the application.

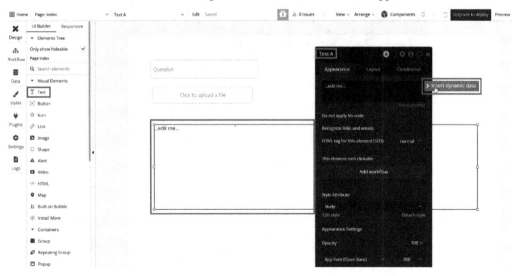

Figure 7.6 – Inserting dynamic data

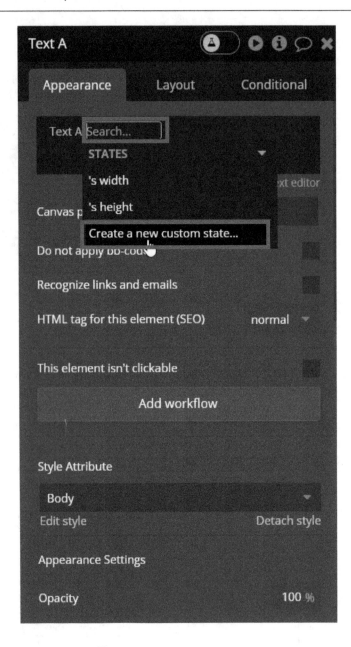

Figure 7.7 – Creating a custom state

20. The next thing we need to do is load the cloud function that we created into Bubble. Select **Plugins** from the left-hand menu and then select **Add Plugins**. Select the **API Connector**, then select **Install**, and then **Done**.

Install New Plugins

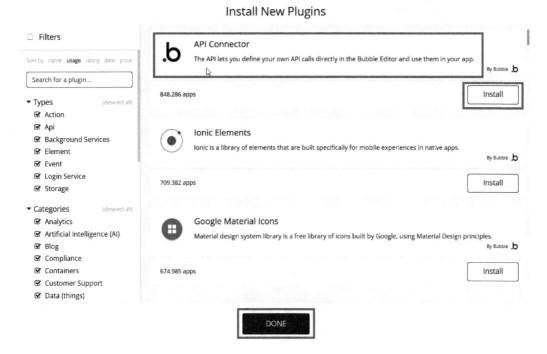

Figure 7.8 – Bubble.io UI configuration

21. Select **API Connector** from the list of plugins. Select **Add Another API**. For the **API name**, type in answer_from_file. Scroll down to **Create a New API** and click **Expand**. Leave the name of this API as API call. For the API, configure the following settings:

- From the **Use as** dropdown menu, select **Action**.

- Change the request from **GET** to **POST**.

- Create a new header by clicking on **New Header**. Select **Add Header**. For **key**, type in Content-Type, and for **value**, type in application/json.

- Add a parameter by clicking **Parameter**. For **key**, type in pdf_url. For **value**, type in https://bookpackt67.blob.core.windows.net/test/ XDroneManual.pdf?sp=r&st=2024-01-12T00:52:16Z&se=2024-12- 31T08:52:16Z&spr=https&sv=2022-11-02&sr=b&sig=IEXLlGXVXCilE g0ffqW8ItXc4LX2YkbRWuZIpSxfP8Y%3D. Do not include any quotes. Ensure that the **private** box is *unchecked*.

- Click on **Parameter** again. For **key**, type in `question`. For **value**, type in `for safety, what's the highest you should fly the drone?`. Do not include any quotes. Ensure that the **private** box is *unchecked*.

22. Select **Initialize Call** to test the API call. If you see the screen shown in *Figure 7.9*, then the call has been successful. Ensure that for each choice, the **text** type has been selected, and click **Save**.

Figure 7.9 – A successful UI configuration

23. Select **Design** from the left-hand menu. Create a Button element by selecting **Button** and then drawing a box below the **File Uploader** element.

24. Double-click the Button element that you have created. In the property menu that appears, select **Add Workflow**.

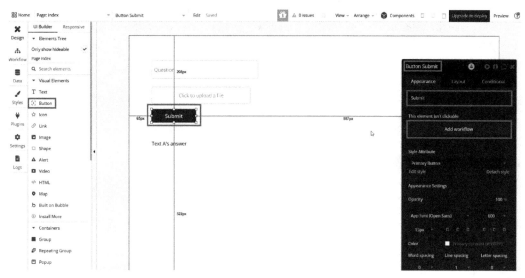

Figure 7.10 – Visual layout of page and adding a workflow

25. Select **Click here to add an action**. Go to **Plugins**, find the API you have just created (`answer_from_file - API call`), and select it. Do the following in the property menu that appears:

- Delete the content of (`param`) `pdf_url`. Type in `http:` and then select **Insert dynamic data**. Scroll down and select **File Uploader A**, and then select **value**.

- Delete the content of (`param`) `question`. Select **Insert dynamic data**. Scroll down and select **Input Question**, and then select **value**.

26. Next, select **Click here to add an action** again, scroll down to **Element Actions**, and then select **Set State**. For the **Element** drop-down menu, select **Text A**. For the **Custom state** drop-down menu, select **answer**. For **Value**, select **Results of step 1** and then select **answer**. This will make the value of **Text A** equal to the answer from the API call to the cloud function that you have created.

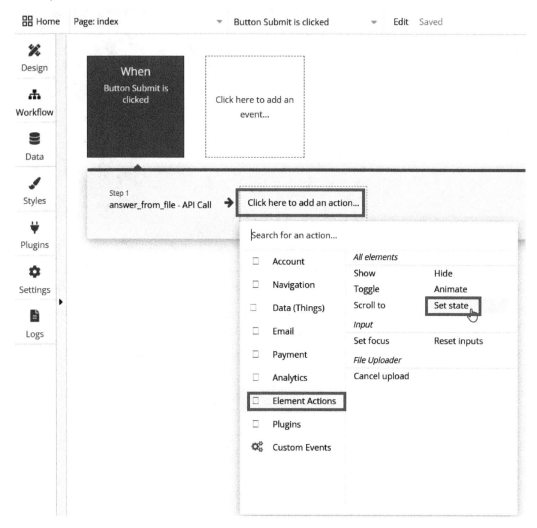

Figure 7.11 – Setting the state in an element

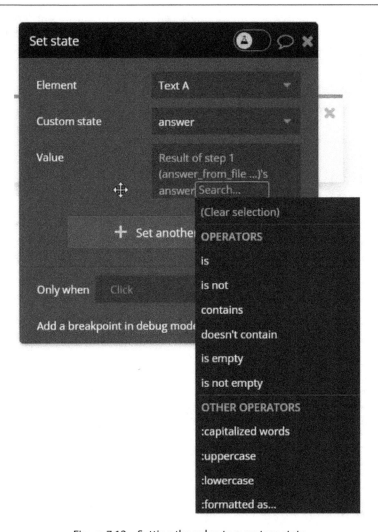

Figure 7.12 – Setting the value to a custom state

27. We have completed everything we need for our Bubble application. Let's test if the application works. Select **Preview** on the right and a new page will appear, with your application. In the **Question** text box, type in `for safety, what's the highest you should fly the drone?`. Select the **File Uploader** input and upload the PDF file of the drone manual that you downloaded earlier.

28. Click the **Submit** button. If all goes well, you should get a screen like the one shown in *Figure 7.13*, which contains the answer to the user's question directly from content in the PDF file.

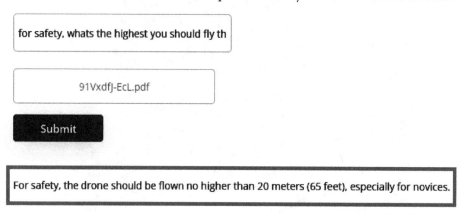

Figure 7.13 – Output from the Bubble application

After you've done this, try typing other questions that are relevant to the PDF file, such as How do I charge the battery? or How do I do a 360 flip?.

How it works...

In this recipe, we created a knowledge-based assistant that can read any PDF file and provide answers to questions based on that file.

This is very similar to the recipes in the previous chapter but with one key difference: the knowledge that is used to answer questions does not come from ChatGPT but instead from a PDF file that was provided.

Code walkthrough

The code that we used in the Google cloud function contains instructions to read the PDF URL, extract the content, and pass it to the OpenAI API, which is what makes this different than previous recipes.

To do this, we had to import two additional Python packages:

- Requests: This package enables us to send HTTP requests easily. This is essential for fetching the PDF file from the provided URL. By using the requests.get() function, we can retrieve the content of any online document, in this case, a PDF file.

- PyPDF2: This package enables us to interact with and manipulate PDF files directly within Python. Once the PDF is fetched, PyPDF2 provides the tools to read the PDF file, extract text, and even handle different aspects of PDF manipulation, if necessary. In our application, it primarily serves to convert the PDF content into a text format that can be processed by the OpenAI API.

We first make a request to the URL of the PDF that is provided to us by the user from the `pdf_url` object. We then convert that into bytes:

```
# Send a GET request to the URL
response = requests.get(pdf_url, stream=True)
response.raise_for_status()  # Ensure the request was successful
```

We then use the `PdfReader` class of `PyPDF2` to read the bytes and read the contents of the PDF file page by page. We save the entire string content of the PDF file to the `text` variable:

```
# save text
text = ''

# Create a PDF reader object using the byte stream from the response
with io.BytesIO(response.content) as pdf_file:
pdf_reader = PdfReader(pdf_file)

    # Iterate over each page and print the text
    for page_num in range(len(pdf_reader.pages)):
        page = pdf_reader.pages[0]
        text = text + page.extract_text()
```

Finally, when we call the OpenAI Chat API, our instructions are for the LLM to read through the text and the user's question, and then to answer the user's question based on the text provided. We then provided the text of the entire PDF file and the user's question:

```
    response = client.chat.completions.create(
    model="gpt-4",
    messages=[
        {
            "role": "system",
            "content": "You are a helpful assistant that goes through text
file and answers questions"
        },
        {
            "role": "user",
            "content": '\n\n TEXT: ' + text + ' \n\n QUESTION: ' + question
        }
    ],
    temperature=0.64,
max_tokens=1000,
top_p=1,
frequency_penalty=0,
```

```
presence_penalty=0
  )


  answer = response.choices[0].message.content
```

This is the same as if you were to go to ChatGPT, copy and paste the content of the entire PDF file, and then ask the user's question. However, in this way, you've built an application around it that makes it far easier for the user – all they need to do is upload the PDF and put their question in a text box.

Limitations of this approach

We have already discussed the benefits: namely that since ChatGPT's internal knowledge may be out of date and it's impossible to track the source of any information provided by ChatGPT, having an architecture that forces the Open API to use only the knowledge provided by the user alleviates this issue.

There are, however, also a few limitations to this approach. It's key to have an understanding of them so you can make the most out of the approach. They are as follows:

- *Dependency on PDF quality*: The accuracy of the assistant is heavily dependent on the quality and clarity of the PDF content. Poorly structured documents or complex formats can lead to incomplete or incorrect responses. Additionally, this method will not work for information embedded within images, as the Open AI API cannot read images.

- *Resource intensity for large documents*: The assistant needs to process and understand the entire document for each query, which can be resource-intensive and result in slow response times, especially for large documents.

- *Limited knowledge scope*: The assistant's knowledge is limited to the specific subject matter of the PDF, lacking the comprehensive coverage found in ChatGPT's built-in database.

- *Maintenance of the knowledge base*: Keeping the information current requires constant updates to the PDF files, which can be time-consuming, especially with frequently changing information.

- *Context window limitation*: The content in the PDF must be within the context window of the ChatGPT model. This approach is not feasible for very long PDFs as the model cannot process content that exceeds its context window (which is the maximum number of words that can be processed by the API), limiting the amount of information that can be used for responses.

As a result, users can adopt another approach that is contained within a special subset of the OpenAI API, called the Assistants API, which we will discuss in the subsequent recipe.

Creating a knowledge-retrieval assistant through the Assistants API

OpenAI has recently released the Assistants API, wherein you can create knowledge-based assistants with minimal coding and complexity. A big advantage is that you can incorporate tools into your assistants that OpenAI has built, such as *Code Interpreter* and *Knowledge Retrieval*. These augmentations essentially give your assistant application superpowers. For this recipe, we will focus on the Knowledge Retrieval tool.

Knowledge Retrieval enhances your assistants by incorporating external knowledge (such as the drone manual PDF file from the previous recipe). OpenAI automatically and efficiently segments any uploaded documents while creating indices of embeddings. These embeddings are stored in OpenAI's database.

Recall in *Chapter 4* we discussed how embeddings can be used to compare text similarity and to search for segments of texts. With Knowledge Retrieval, OpenAI does this automatically for you. When a user asks the Assistants API a question that is augmented by Knowledge Retrieval, it employs a vector search to extract pertinent information from the uploaded documents, responding effectively to user inquiries.

In this way, the knowledge source can be infinite in length, as the knowledge source itself is not passed to the Chat API, but instead is vectorized and only small relevant segments of text are passed to the Chat API based on a user's question.

In other words, using the Assistants API with Knowledge Retrieval means that you can upload large PDFs and as many PDFs as you want, and there is effectively no context window limitation.

This is useful for creating highly specialized assistants that need to draw on vast amounts of specific information. For instance, if you're building an assistant for legal professionals, you can upload numerous legal texts, case studies, and statutes. The Assistants API, powered by Knowledge Retrieval, can then provide precise legal references and interpretations in response to complex queries. Similarly, for medical professionals, uploading extensive medical literature and research papers enables the Assistants API to offer detailed medical insights. This makes the Assistants API not just a conversational tool, but a robust, information-rich resource.

In this recipe, we will use the Assistants API to create a *Legal Constitution Helper* assistant that gets its knowledge directly from the US Constitution document.

How to do it...

Playground

1. Navigate to `https://openai.com`. Select **Playground** from the left-hand menu. In the top menu, ensure that **Assistants** is selected from the drop-down menu. Select the dropdown near the top and select **Create assistant** to create a new assistant.

2. Enter the following configuration details for **Assistant**:

   - **Name:** `US Constitution Expert`.

   - **Instructions:** `You are a helpful assistant that helps answer legal constitution related questions from reading the US constitution. Reference specific parts of the document where you found the information required to answer the question.`

   - **Model: gpt-4-1106-preview**.

   - Toggle the **Retrieval** tool *on*.

   - Under **Files**, select **Add**, and upload the following file (`https://bookpackt67.blob.core.windows.net/test/us_constitution.pdf?sp=r&st=2024-01-15T07:51:23Z&se=2024-12-31T15:51:23Z&spr=https&sv=2022-11-02&sr=b&sig=C9hFIvrI3FHogBumPTRaL1hrwS8C1B0t3hn1zS9t6Ew%3D`). This file is the US Constitution.

> **Note**
>
> You will need to download the file locally to then upload it to OpenAI.

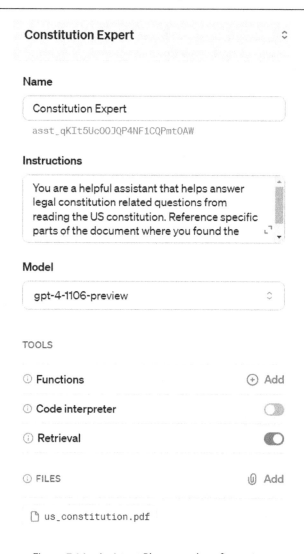

Figure 7.14 – Assistant Playground configuration

3. Select the **Save** button at the bottom. After you do this, an assistant ID will appear directly below the **Name** field. It will be in the following format: *asst_XXXXXXXXXXXXXXXXXXXXXX*. Note this down, as this is the unique ID for your assistant, and we will need to reference this in the backend function that we create.

Google Cloud Functions

4. In a new tab, navigate to `https://cloud.google.com` and log in with your Google credentials.

5. Select **Console** in the top right.

6. Create a new Google cloud function. In the search bar, type in function, select **Cloud Functions**, and then select **Create Function**.

7. Name the function a descriptive name. We are going to aptly name it get_answer.

8. In the **Authentication** menu, ensure that you select **Allow unauthenticated invocations** as the authentication method. This will enable the frontend application to make calls to the backend layer.

9. Select the **Runtime, build, connections and security settings** drop-down menu to expand the options. Change **timeout** from 60 seconds to 300 seconds. This will make sure that the timeout for the Google cloud function is not 1 minute but five minutes instead.

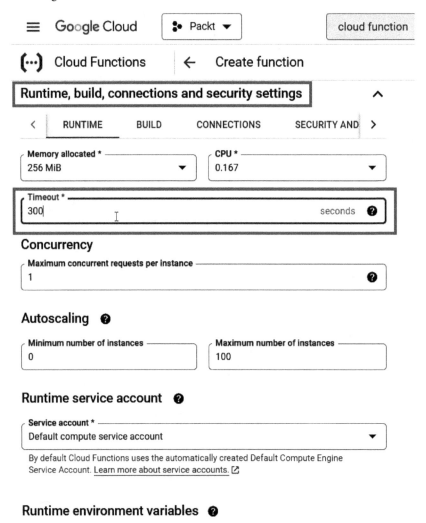

Figure 7.15 – Google cloud function configuration settings

10. Select **Next** to move on to function development. In the **Runtime** dropdown menu, select **Python 3.12**. For **entry point**, select or type in **get_answer**.

11. Go to `Requirements.txt` in the left-hand menu and type the following Python package in as this library will be used in the backend function:

```
openai
```

12. For the actual code block, type in the following. This function takes in one input (`question`) and returns the relevant `answer` through the Assistants API. The code walkthrough will be discussed in the *Using the assistant* sub-section. Replace the `<assistant-id-here>` with the assistant ID you noted down in *step 3* of the *Playground* section:

```python
import functions_framework
import time
from openai import OpenAI

@functions_framework.http
def get_answer(request):

  # declare assistant id
assistant_id = '<assistant-id-here>'

  # get inputs
request_json = request.get_json(silent=True)
  question = request_json['question']

  # initializeopenai
  client = OpenAI(api_key = '<api-key here>')

  # create a thread
  thread = client.beta.threads.create()

  # create message question in thread
  message = client.beta.threads.messages.create(
thread_id=thread.id,
    role="user",
    content=question
    )

  # run assistant
  run = client.beta.threads.runs.create(
thread_id=thread.id,
assistant_id=assistant_id,
  instructions=""
```

```
    )

    # wait 30 seconds for response
  time.sleep(30)

    # get answer
  thread_messages = client.beta.threads.messages.list(thread.id)
    answer = thread_messages.data[0].content[0].text.value

    # return answer
    result = {
      'answer': answer
    }

    return result
```

13. Select **Deploy**. You might need to wait five minutes for the deployment to fully complete. When you see the green checkmark on the cloud function screen, your function has been successfully deployed.

14. Similar to the previous recipe, we will now use Postman to test the cloud function that we have just deployed. Open **Postman**. Select **New** on the top left, select **HTTP**.

15. In the Postman request, select **Headers** and type in a new header, with the **Key** equal to `Content-Type` and the **value** equal to `application/json`.

16. Change the request from **Get** to **Post** from the left-hand drop-down menu. Copy the endpoint URL from the **Cloud Function** page and paste it into Postman.

17. Select **Body**, then select **Raw**, and copy and paste the following JSON request:

```
  {
      "question": "How many senators are there?"
  }
```

18. Select **Send** to make the call to your cloud function. If all goes well, you should see an answer such as this:

```
The Senate of the United States shall be composed of two
Senators from each state, and each Senator shall have one vote.
```

Bubble

19. Navigate to w and log in. Select **Create an app** and give your app a relevant name. Select **Get started** and then select **Start with basic features**. You can also click the **Skip the Application Assistant** prompt if you encounter it.

20. On the Canvas page, we are going to add a few elements that are required for our application. Select **Input** from the left-hand menu and then draw a rectangle at the top of the page. Double-click the element and on the property menu, replace **Placeholder** with `question`.

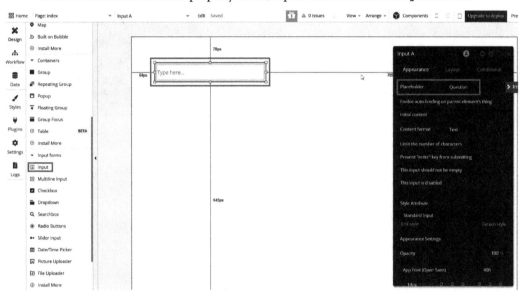

Figure 7.16 – Bubble input configuration

21. Next, create a text element by selecting it from the left-hand menu and drawing a rectangle (make it multiple lines) directly below the previous elements. Double-click the text element to show the property. Then, click **insert dynamic data** on the actual text field, select **Text A**, and select **create a new custom state**. You will be prompted for a name and type. For the name, type in `answer`. For the type, ensure **text** is selected. This will create a unique custom state for the text box, which is required to show the values in the application.

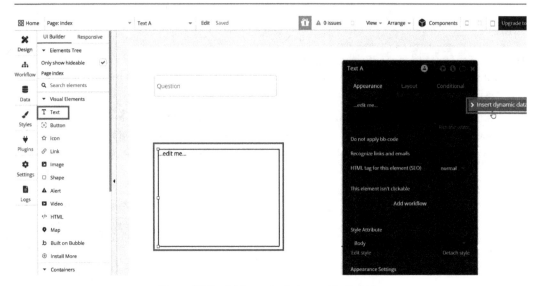

Figure 7.17 – Adding a text element to Bubble

22. The next thing we need to do is to load the cloud function that we created into Bubble. Select **Plugins** from the left-hand menu, and then select **Add Plugins**. Select the **API Connector**, and then select **Install**, and then **Done**.

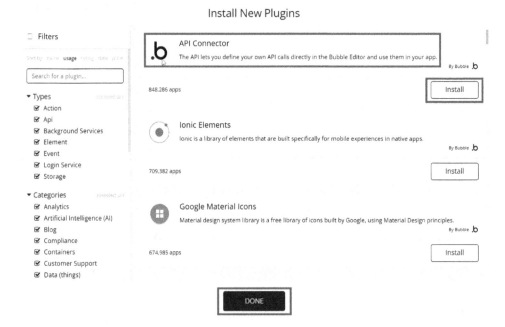

Figure 7.18 – Bubble.io UI configuration

23. Select **API Connector** from the list of plugins. Select **Add Another API**. For the **API name**, type in `get_answer`. Scroll down to **Create a New API**, and click **Expand**. Leave the name of this API to `API call`. For the API, configure the settings to the following:

   - From the **Use as** drop-down menu, select **Action**.

   - Change request from **GET** to **POST**.

   - Create a new header using **New Header**. Select **Add Header.** For **key** type in `Content-Type` for **value** type in `application/json`.

   - Click on **Parameter** to add a parameter. For **key**, type in `question`. For **value**, type in How many senators are there?. Do not include any quotes. Ensure that the **private** box is *unchecked*.

24. Select **Initialize Call** to test the API call. Ensure that for each **choice**, the **text** type has been selected, and click **Save**.

25. Select **Design** from left-hand menu. Create a Button element by selecting **Button** and then drawing a box to the right of the Input element.

26. Double-click the **Button** element that you had created. In the property menu that appears, select **Add Workflow**.

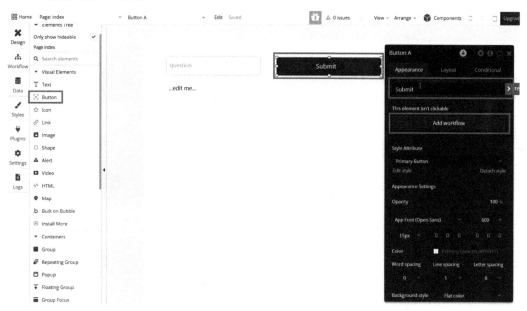

Figure 7.19 – Visual layout of page and adding a button and a workflow

27. Select **Click here to add an action**. Go to **Plugins** and find the API you had just created (`get_answer - API call`) and select it. In the property menu that appears, delete the content of (`param`) `question`. Select **Insert dynamic data**. Scroll down, select **Input Question**, and then select **value**.

28. Next, select **Click here to add an action** again, scroll down to **Element Actions**, and then select **Set State**. For the **Element** drop-down menu, select **Text A**. For the **Custom state** drop-down menu, select **answer**. For **Value**, select **Results of step 1** and then select **answer**. This will make the value of **Text A** equal to the answer from the API call to the cloud function that you created.

29. We have completed everything we need for our Bubble application. Let's test whether the application works. Select **Preview** on the right and a new page will appear, with your application. In the **Question** text box, type in How many senators are there?.

30. Select the **Submit** button. If all goes well, you should get an answer similar to the one you saw before in Postman, which answers the question with text from the *US Constitution document* that we uploaded earlier.

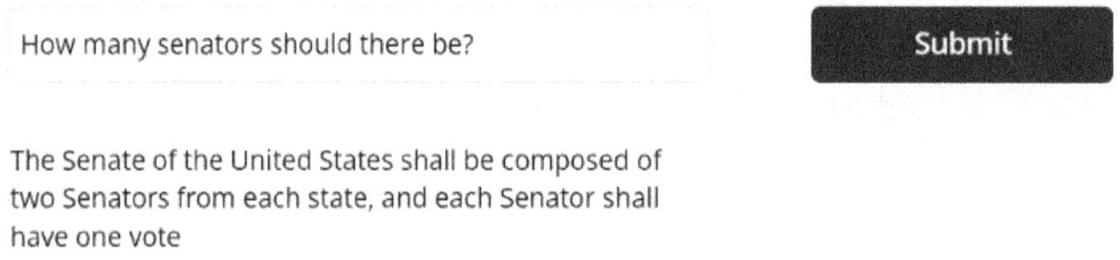

How many senators should there be?   Submit

The Senate of the United States shall be composed of
two Senators from each state, and each Senator shall
have one vote

Figure 7.20 – Bubble application example question

The best part about this is that you can ask *any* related question and it will answer based on the US Constitution document that you uploaded, even if it was several hundred pages. The answers are also document-specific. For example, you can ask How old must a person be to become a Senator? and it'll generate a response, as shown in *Figure 7.21*.

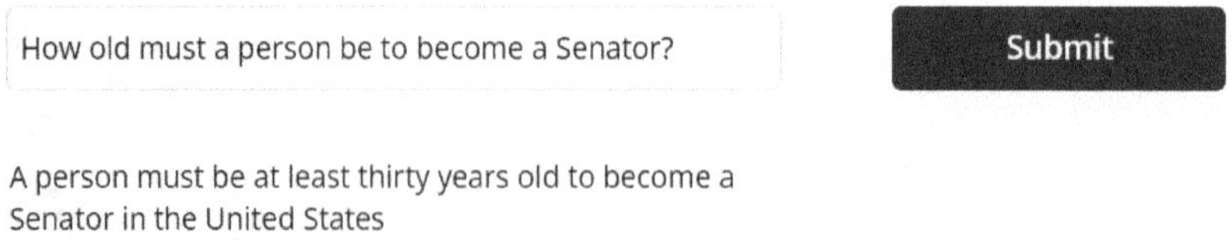

How old must a person be to become a Senator?   Submit

A person must be at least thirty years old to become a
Senator in the United States

Figure 7.21 – Bubble application example question

You can see in *Figure 7.22* that the PDF uses different language, but the assistant has reworked it to match the format of the question that we asked.

> No Person shall be a Senator who shall not have attained to the Age of thirty Years, and been nine Years a Citizen of the United States, and who shall not, when elected, be an Inhabitant of that State for which he shall be chosen.
>
> The Vice President of the United States shall be President of the Senate, but shall have no Vote, unless they be equally divided.

Figure 7.22 – Document excerpt from where the answer is retrieved

How it works...

In this recipe, we created an assistant that answers questions from a PDF that we loaded in.

The handbook is 85 pages long and contains over 35,000 words, and yet the API has no issues with finding the right information from the handbook. It is worth noting that this could have been done with a knowledge source that is a million words, or several large PDF files. That is the beauty of the Retrieval tool within the Assistants API – it can scale very easily.

Creating the assistant

We created the assistant using the **OpenAI Playground** instead of through the OpenAI API. The OpenAI Playground provides a nice UI for creating our initial assistant instead of having to build using code. We defined the following parameters when building our assistant:

- **Name**: The name of the assistant.

- **Instructions**: The system instructions that the assistant uses. This is very similar to the System Message that was used in the Chat API.

- **Model**: The Chat model to use when constructing answers. For assistants, GPT-4 is always recommended due to its ability to understand and answer nuanced information, a critical element in any knowledge-retrieval application.

- **Tools**: Superpowers that can be added to your assistant. We added the Retrieval tool, which again enables OpenAI to read through and search knowledge bases that the user uploads.

- **Files**: A set of files to upload that will be used as the knowledge source.

Using the assistant

In the **Google** cloud function, we first create a message thread with the user's question:

```
# create a thread
  thread = client.beta.threads.create()

# create message question in thread
message = client.beta.threads.messages.create(
thread_id=thread.id,
    role="user",
    content=question
    )
```

We then run the assistant, providing the unique *assistant ID* that is generated when we create the assistant in the OpenAI playground, and the *thread ID* of the message thread that contains that user question.

Note that after running the assistant, we force our function to sleep for 30 seconds. We do this because we need to give the assistant time to fully process the message thread. Another way to do this would be to poll the assistant in a loop and progress only once the poll shows a successful completion. If you'd like to know more about this method, you can go to https://pypi.org/project/polling2/:

```
# run assistant
run = client.beta.threads.runs.create(
thread_id=thread.id,
assistant_id=assistant_id,
    instructions=""
    )

# wait 30 seconds for response
time.sleep(30)
```

We then extract the assistant's reply and return the message as the `answer`:

```
# get answer
thread_messages = client.beta.threads.messages.list(thread.id)
    answer = thread_messages.data[0].content[0].text.value

# return answer
result = {
    'answer': answer
    }
```

Other use cases

The combination of the Assistants API and the Retrieval tool offers a wide array of potential applications across various industries and domains. Here are some examples:

- *Customer support chatbots*: Develop chatbots that can provide detailed and specific answers to customer queries by accessing a company's extensive knowledge base or product manuals

- *Healthcare information systems*: Build systems that can retrieve and provide specific medical information, guidelines, or research papers to healthcare professionals, aiding in diagnosis or treatment decisions

- *Legal research assistants*: Create tools that can sift through large volumes of legal documents, cases, and precedents to assist lawyers in preparing for cases or conducting legal research

- *Educational platforms*: Develop educational aids that can pull information from textbooks, research papers, or educational materials to assist students in learning or researching various topics

- *Financial advisory tools*: Build applications that can access and analyze financial reports, market trends, and economic research to provide investment advice or market insights

- *Technical support and troubleshooting*: Implement systems that can access technical manuals and user guides to provide step-by-step troubleshooting assistance or technical guidance

- *Content curation and recommendation systems*: Create platforms that can analyze and retrieve articles, news, or multimedia content based on user preferences or queries

- *Corporate data retrieval systems*: Develop internal tools for businesses that can search through corporate documents, reports, and databases to provide employees with quick access to the information they need

- *Travel and hospitality assistants*: Build travel assistants that can access and provide information on travel destinations, accommodations, local customs, or points of interest

- *E-commerce personal shopping assistants*: Create tools that can recommend products based on user queries by searching through product catalogs and reviews

Each of these applications uses the capabilities of the Assistants API to understand and process natural language queries and the Retrieval tool's ability to access and extract relevant information from a vast array of documents and data sources. This combination enables the creation of powerful, context-aware, and highly informative applications.

As we wrap up our journey through the expansive world of the OpenAI API, I hope you feel empowered to harness its capabilities to fuel your innovative projects. From taking those initial steps in setting up your API environment to exploring the intricate details of endpoints and key parameters, we've traversed a path that has prepared you to not just understand but to also apply the OpenAI API in creating applications that can transform the way we interact with technology. The exploration of additional features and the process of staging and hosting for application development have laid down the foundation for you to build intelligent solutions that can make a difference.

Whether it's designing versatile intelligent applications or crafting knowledge-based assistants, the skills you've garnered are a testament to the potential that lies in your hands. Remember, the journey doesn't end here. Each application you build is a step towards innovation, a bridge to solving complex problems, and a contribution to a future where technology and human creativity converge in harmony. Embrace the challenges and opportunities that come your way, for you are now equipped to make a significant impact in the world of technology.

Index

www.packtpub.com

Subscribe to our online digital library for full access to over 7,000 books and videos, as well as industry leading tools to help you plan your personal development and advance your career. For more information, please visit our website.

Why subscribe?

- Spend less time learning and more time coding with practical eBooks and Videos from over 4,000 industry professionals

- Improve your learning with Skill Plans built especially for you

- Get a free eBook or video every month

- Fully searchable for easy access to vital information

- Copy and paste, print, and bookmark content

Did you know that Packt offers eBook versions of every book published, with PDF and ePub files available? You can upgrade to the eBook version at www.packtpub.com and as a print book customer, you are entitled to a discount on the eBook copy. Get in touch with us at customercare@packtpub.com for more details.

At www.packtpub.com, you can also read a collection of free technical articles, sign up for a range of free newsletters, and receive exclusive discounts and offers on Packt books and eBooks.

Other Books You May Enjoy

If you enjoyed this book, you may be interested in these other books by Packt:

The Future of Finance with ChatGPT and Power BI

James Bryant, Aloke Mukherjee

ISBN: 978-1-80512-334-7

- Dominate investing, trading, and reporting with ChatGPT's game-changing insights

- Master Power BI for dynamic financial visuals, custom dashboards, and impactful charts

- Apply AI and ChatGPT for advanced finance analysis and natural language processing (NLP) in news analysis

- Tap into ChatGPT for powerful market sentiment analysis to seize investment opportunities

- Unleash your financial analysis potential with data modeling, source connections, and Power BI integration

- Understand the importance of data security and adopt best practices for using ChatGPT and Power BI

Building AI Applications with ChatGPT APIs

Martin Yanev

ISBN: 978-1-80512-756-7

- Develop a solid foundation in using the ChatGPT API for natural language processing tasks
- Build, deploy, and capitalize on a variety of desktop and SaaS AI applications
- Seamlessly integrate ChatGPT with established frameworks such as Flask, Django, and Microsoft Office APIs
- Channel your creativity by integrating DALL-E APIs to produce stunning AI-generated art within your desktop applications
- Experience the power of Whisper API's speech recognition and text-to-speech features
- Discover techniques to optimize ChatGPT models through the process of fine-tuning

Packt is searching for authors like you

If you're interested in becoming an author for Packt, please visit `authors.packtpub.com` and apply today. We have worked with thousands of developers and tech professionals, just like you, to help them share their insight with the global tech community. You can make a general application, apply for a specific hot topic that we are recruiting an author for, or submit your own idea.

Share Your Thoughts

Now you've finished *OpenAI API Cookbook*, we'd love to hear your thoughts! Scan the QR code below to go straight to the Amazon review page for this book and share your feedback or leave a review on the site that you purchased it from.

https://packt.link/r/1805121359

Your review is important to us and the tech community and will help us make sure we're delivering excellent quality content.

Download a free PDF copy of this book

Thanks for purchasing this book!

Do you like to read on the go but are unable to carry your print books everywhere?

Is your eBook purchase not compatible with the device of your choice?

Don't worry, now with every Packt book you get a DRM-free PDF version of that book at no cost.

Read anywhere, any place, on any device. Search, copy, and paste code from your favorite technical books directly into your application.

The perks don't stop there, you can get exclusive access to discounts, newsletters, and great free content in your inbox daily

Follow these simple steps to get the benefits:

1. Scan the QR code or visit the link below

https://packt.link/free-ebook/9781805121350

2. Submit your proof of purchase
3. That's it! We'll send your free PDF and other benefits to your email directly

www.ingramcontent.com/pod-product-compliance
Lightning Source LLC
LaVergne TN
LVHW081526050326
832903LV00025B/1640